NATALIE SISSON

The Suitcase

ENTREPRENEUR

CREATE FREEDOM IN BUSINESS AND ADVENTURE IN LIFE

Copyeditor: Matthew Kimberley
Cover Design: Alexander von Ness
Interior and Back Cover Design: Cheryl Wood

First published in 2013.

Published by Tonawhai Press.
ISBN 978-0-473-25124-6

To my wonderful parents
Peter and Gina and
my sister Debbie.
I'm truly the luckiest
daughter and sister
on this planet. Here's to
many more adventures
together.

Contents

INTRODUCTION

Choosing your own adventure 5

Why I wrote this book and who I wrote it for 7

Act 1

Welcome to the new world of digital nomads 11

CHAPTER 1

My story–from broke to $15,000 in one month 15

CHAPTER 2

The only four things you need to be free 31

CHAPTER 3

Real stories of others living life on their own terms 43

Act 2

How to build an online business you can take anywhere 61

CHAPTER 4

The future of work and why there is no better time than now
to build your own business 63

CHAPTER 5

Building an online business for your Suitcase Entrepreneur lifestyle 83

CHAPTER 6

Becoming a citizen of the world and setting up an
international business 105

CHAPTER 7

The best systems and online tools to run your business from anywhere 123

CHAPTER 8

How to use social media as your marketing, sales and customer service team 139

CHAPTER 9

How to build a world-class team you may never meet 161

Act 3

How on earth does one become a Suitcase Entrepreneur? 183

CHAPTER 10

How to become a pro at being homeless 187

CHAPTER 11

Deciding on where to travel and your preparation checklist 213

CHAPTER 12

The art of minimalism and how to pack for anywhere 237

CHAPTER 13

Travel hacking tips and tools to save you time and money 253

CONCLUSION

Choosing freedom in business and adventure in life 287

RESOURCES

Your go-to directory 293

ABOUT THE AUTHOR 309

ACKNOWLEDGEMENTS 311

Introduction

Choosing your own adventure.

The Universe rewards bravery –
stop making excuses and get to it.
~NATALIE SISSON

My friends thought I was mad buying a one-way ticket to Canada, to chase my dreams of working for myself, especially since I'd just got a raise at work and had bought an apartment in London, England.

But quitting that lucrative 9-5 job and jumping on a plane seemed like a completely logical thing to do in order to discover a new way of living.

That was in 2008 and the journey to achieving freedom in my business and adventure in my life since then has been one big unconventional roller-coaster … and I wouldn't change a minute of it.

Sure, there were plenty of moments of doubt, of fear, of questioning my sanity. But they only showed me that I was living life to the full and pushing my boundaries.

In this book I've set out to prove to you that you can live life exactly how you want to and to show you what's possible.

I believe that there's no better time than right now to live life on your own terms and I'm on a mission to inspire you to build a business and a life that you love, using just a laptop, smartphone and an Internet connection.

It's never been easier and more affordable to build a business from any-where using online tools, social media, outsourcing and a lot of hustle.

What's more, you can choose to do this while living wherever you want in the world, whether that's your hometown, another country or even from your suitcase.

I should know. After 9 years in the corporate world I've built a six-figure global business from nothing with just a blog and close to zero investment. Now I travel the world, living out of my suitcase and teach others how to do the same.

So sit back, return your seatback to the upright position, switch off your mobile phone and prepare for take off.

Why I wrote this book and who I wrote it for.

Do not follow where the path may lead.
Go instead where there is no path and leave a trail
~ RALPH WALDO EMERSON

Everybody has the right to create freedom in business and live life on their own terms and that's what this book will teach you to do. I'm not expecting you to do exactly what I do and live out of a suitcase, but I am expecting you to want to live life on your own terms.

That's why I wrote this book; to ensure you have the tools and know-how to live the life you dream of, whether that's drinking Mai Tais on a tropical island while creating digital products, or running a horse-training business via Skype and YouTube from your local café.

I built my business and community out of nothing but a blog and a desire and determination to fit my work around my dream lifestyle. Not the other way around.

A novel idea

As you can probably tell, I like to buck convention. I was never good with people telling me I couldn't do something; that just made me more determined to prove them wrong.

So, at first, when I was asked to write a book by a big name' traditional publisher, I couldn't believe it! I jumped up and down like an excited kid! I'd always wanted to write a book and this felt like my permission slip.

I wrote the book proposal using their template, but then they turned it down, saying *"people aren't ready for completely virtual businesses, Natalie."* I remember laughing out loud, incredulous, and wondering if they'd read the *4-Hour Workweek*, which had come out 5 years earlier.

People all around me were catching on to this virtual business revolution and location-independence was becoming a common phrase. If I waited another year to write this book, it would already be too late.

Then it struck me. Why on earth was I considering going the traditional route, giving away all my control, content rights and the majority of my profits, to a publisher stuck in dying industry model? Especially one that didn't understand me, or likely, where I was coming from.

This was just the same scenario as working in a 9-5 job, for people that gave me no freedom to make an impact on the world, and bring my art to those who needed it most.

So I used the very online tools that helped me build my business in the first place to self-publish this book.

That's right: this book was paid for and supported through a Kickstarter campaign. Close to 200 people pledged their support, essentially saying, '*Natalie we want to see this book written*'.

It's been read and lovingly improved by those who pledged to be on the editorial team, and the three sections that make up the backbone of this book were from generous sponsor level pledges through Kickstarter too.

I think this is the perfect example of how we can do things on our own terms; of how the world is changing, and it proves you can do just about anything you put your mind to, even if you don't have much money.

You can choose your own adventure and make it a reality by harnessing the power of people, online tools, technology and social media to change the way in which we do business.

Why you should read this book

I want this book to challenge your current way of thinking and show you that becoming a digital nomad is within your grasp, if you truly want it.

You don't need:

- An office to run your business

- A permanent residential address to live at

- To work traditional business hours – ever

- Your team to be present or even in the same country or time zone

- To meet your clients or customers face to face

- More than $100 or 24 hours to start your online business

- An excuse to travel or to live in just one place.

- Permission to do what you want when you want and live a full life.

Who is this book for?

It's for you if you want to quit your job and create your own path to freedom, whether from your own home, or some exotic location on the other side of the world.

It's for you, the business owner, who's working hard to build a profitable company that makes an impact, but you want the freedom and flexibility on when and where to run it from.

It's also for you if you're an employee who wants to go traveling, and then come back to sell your services to the very company you left behind.

How should you read it?

If you're just starting out on the road of entrepreneurship or you need the motivation to quit your job, then I suggest you start at the very beginning, and read how others have achieved their ideal lifestyle, including my journey.

If you're already in business, or on the verge of it, and wanting to free up more time and not be bound to one location, then skip to Act 2 to tap into the different business models to make this possible, and the key tools and technology available to you, to make it happen.

If you're curious about how to pack up your life and business and go jet-setting around the world, or at least on a more regular basis, then jump straight to Act 3.

There are many links provided throughout this book to references, tools and services that you will find as invaluable as I have. I've also created an entire online resource section for readers that you can access anytime and will be constantly updated with the latest and greatest at **suitcaseentrepreneur.com/book/resources**.

Let the journey begin.

Act 1

Welcome to the new world of digital nomads.

A journey of a thousand miles must begin with a single step.
~ LAO TZU

Life as we know it has fundamentally changed, and anything and everything you think is normal will be challenged in upcoming years. Freedom is the new currency, and by that I mean, if you can monetize yourself, your skills, or those of others, you can be both fulfilled and financially free.

The future is bright and it belongs to the digital nomads, online marketers and knowledge providers who make valuable content accessible in numerous formats and available any time from almost any device. That's the kind of person I am. And it's the kind of person you can be, too.

"The decision to become a Lifestyle Entrepreneur flows directly from the first and most important decision — to become an Entrepreneur. Fourteen years ago I had an idea for the world's first accurate, strapless, heart rate watch. What a terrific idea!

No more sweaty, uncomfortable chest straps! I thought my watch — the MIO — would change the world. I left a comfortable corporate career with visions of early retirement — sailboats, beaches and most importantly — time for myself and my family.

I thought I would quickly get to the end of the road. But, soon it became very clear; the end was a long way away. Fast forward to today and I'm still on that road. It's taken more than a few turns; some directly backward — but I'm loving every minute of it.

An idea is just that, an idea. Turning an idea into a thriving business is typically one of those twenty year "overnight" success stories. So, before jumping straight in, make sure your business is connected intimately with your passion.

A study of successful entrepreneurs found three key traits:

- Responding positively to all challenges and learning from mistakes

- Taking personal initiative

- Having great perseverance.

What this tells you is the road is hard, long and bumpy. You and the business necessarily become inseparable. To preserve your mental health you have to absolutely love your work. Then, your work becomes your play, and you never tire of it.

The "lifestyle" part for me is having the discipline not to overwork. Be sure to set boundaries for yourself and your family so they respect and expect that you have to work, but live up to your commitment that when it's time to play — you will play!

Being an Entrepreneur has allowed me more freedom than a regular job. I go on great, long family vacations; run my dog 5km/day; usually say good-bye to my son in the morning before school, and hello when he gets home again, all while inventing and selling serious products, like **MIO ALPHA**, that have profoundly impacted fitness training. I have never been healthier or had a better lifestyle — and I have never worked harder in my life."

Liz Dickinson Founder of MIO Global, and proud sponsor of Act 1.

Chapter 1

My story – from broke to $15,000 in one month.

Life is either a daring adventure or nothing.
~HELEN KELLER

M y working day is a little … different. I don't go to an office. I rarely, if ever, go to meetings. Although I run my own business that allows me to travel all over the world, my schedule is mine to do with as I choose.

And I don't choose boardrooms, clock-watching, time-stamping or those endless grey meetings in grey boardrooms with grey, desperately unhappy people.

Since you are reading this, then I bet that's not the life for you, either.

Instead, you want to spend your days like I do: cycling through Africa, throwing yourself off the Victoria Falls Bridge, Zambia, riding a motorbike through the hills of Thailand or hiking the famous W Trail in Patagonia.

That's what I do, and all while my business works for me. The good news is: you can do the same. You can run a thriving online business from your laptop, from anywhere in the world, on your own schedule.

Let me show you how.

Here's my secret

I choose **freedom** as my highest value in life. I do everything in my power to have more of it. This means that every single decision I make is based upon staying true to this value. If it doesn't fit, I don't do it.

In pursuit of freedom I have become a homeless vagabond (or world citizen) and live out of my suitcase full-time. I have no address and no home base, but I do have the ability to truly live life on my own terms.

There are two types of reactions when I tell people what I do.

The first is "Wow! That sounds amazing. I'd love to be able to do that one day."

The second is "Are you crazy?" followed by "Don't you have an actual home? How on earth do you manage that?"

So am I crazy? Perhaps a little – I'll let you be the judge.

Who is Natalie Sisson?

I grew up in New Zealand, one of the most beautiful countries in the world, where my European parents had settled after a world tour honeymoon.

I spent my childhood outdoors, playing sport. Dad worked hard so we could enjoy as many vacations as his job – as an insurance salesman – would allow.

I started to travel with the family at the age of two. By the time I turned six, I ended up having to repeat a school year due to our family having taken too much time off to travel!

Fast forward to age 27 and I was still struck with the travel bug. In fact, I found myself with a strong urge to leave New Zealand … possibly indefinitely. I packed my bags in February 2006 and spent the next 300 days living out of a suitcase.

In fact, I've been in a permanent state of pack ever since.

I started by traveling across South East Asia and ended up arriving in London, England on my 27th birthday where I stayed for 2.5 years. Since then I've also called Vancouver, Buenos Aires, Los Angeles, Amsterdam and Berlin home (even if just for a few months).

On top of all of these nomadic pursuits I have managed to build a successful online business and a movement of Suitcase Entrepreneurs that I'm privileged to lead.

Leaving traditional work behind

If you're wondering how on earth I achieved this, then know that it all comes down to one simple philosophy:

A true desire to live my life the way I want to, no matter what.

This true desire is what people are missing as they detail all the reasons they can't possibly live the life they want.

My way of living hasn't always been like this. I spent close to nine years of my life chasing the corporate dream, working my way up through high-paying jobs in marketing, brand management and business development across a diverse range of industries in both New Zealand and Europe.

Working for someone else really taught me important lessons about what works and what doesn't, especially from an operations and management perspective.

Looking back, I always chose roles where I was offered a lot of scope and flexibility to work on my own initiatives, and where I was able to take charge of making them happen. This was a good thing because I hate authority. Most managers realized this quickly, but not before they had hired me.

I am a self-motivated person and often started in a defined role only to turn it upside down. A 9-month contract with a global pharmaceutical company saw me travel all over Europe, working with key opinion leaders and local sales teams, but also saw me reinvent its entire brand positioning including the core message, marketing collateral and communication strategy. This 'take the bull by the horns' approach earned me a lot of respect and a big bonus.

By June 2008 though, I had had enough of the 9-to-5. My high-level job in London, where I was at the time, pushed me over the edge. On paper it looked amazing: great pay, head of a brand new department, the ability to build my own team …

… but it was with an old school firm which was archaic in its thinking, smothered in bureaucracy and drowning in office politics. My lack of progress was slowly killing me. I was battling against the very people who had hired me to do the job!

So less than a year after starting that particular job just after having received a raise and a solid performance review, I quit.

My friends thought I was crazy, as I'd just bought a house in London too. But I was sick and tired of working in organizations where I had no freedom to make a real impact or to influence the outcome.

Fixing my entrepreneurial wings

Less than two weeks after quitting in London, I bought a one-way plane ticket to Vancouver (Canada), represented New Zealand at the Ultimate Frisbee Championships and started a new life.

I had invested most of my final salary payout and pension plan into my property but had enough money left in the bank for just a few months living costs in Vancouver – one of the most expensive cities in the world.

Lesson 1: *To make a real change you need to get uncomfortable*

If you're going to make a significant change in your life, consider making a big move like taking a trip to a different part of the world, or at least to a new location within your country. This helps you to get out of your comfort zone and take a different perspective. After all, "if you do what you've always done, you'll get what you've always got."

After my 9-5 experiences in the corporate world, I was determined to start my own business in my own way and so was hitting up every networking event available in order to make strong connections. As luck would have it, I met my future business partner — Daryl Hatton — at one of these events.

Our respective loves of marketing and technology brought us together two days later when we discussed his idea to build a social fundraising platform. He told me that when I said "I'm a homeless unemployed bum and I want to start my own business" that he was sold! (Well, that, and my solid background in marketing and business development, which complemented his technology background perfectly.)

Lesson 2: Know your special sauce

When I ask people what it is that they do better than anyone else, I often see them pause and think. If you want to take advantage of all the opportunities available to you, you have to know what it is that sets you apart: your 'Special Sauce'.

You may be excellent at building relationships, or founding teams, or making the complex seem simple, or breaking large projects down into manageable chunks. You may 'just' be really good at listening, talking or socializing. All of these talents can be your strategic advantage. But more than that, you need to be able to communicate this clearly and effectively to everyone you meet, in a heartbeat. The better you can define what your unique ingredient is and how it can be applied in the situation you're in, the more opportunities will come your way.

Daryl and I joined forces in September 2008 and formed ConnectionPoint Systems. At about this time I was starting to get a little desperate for funds, having been in Vancouver for a few months already and burning through my savings.

We set to work creating FundRazr, which — due in no part to me — is now the number one fundraising application on Facebook with more than a million users.

While Daryl was a seasoned entrepreneur, I was thrown into the deep end. My time was spent getting to grips with the world of alpha and beta releases, speaking the language of developers, figuring out how to make money when 'freemium' was all the rage and understanding the world of angel investors so that we could actually survive on our current burn rate (how much cash you spend each month when building a company from scratch).

My way of dealing with being in the male-dominated technology industry, and understanding the entire spectrum of being involved in a startup, was to blog about it. It was a cathartic experience for me to write about all that I was learning, on a weekly basis.

I set up a WordPress site, bought the domain name WomanzWorld.com and set about learning all I could about blogging.

Meanwhile, our team worked on the standard startup diet of little sleep, long hours and too much caffeine. We were strapped financially, which meant the pressure was on to ship our product to market as soon as we could.

After an intense period of building our application and finding investors, both Daryl and I started to realize that I was more into my blog than our startup. Eighteen months after starting this company, and with Daryl's blessing, I left to pursue my *own thing*.

The trouble was I had no idea what that *thing* was.

Lesson 3: Don't wait for the right time

Even if you're naturally risk-averse, throw yourself in the deep end if you really want to change your current circumstances. Nothing makes you move heaven and earth to get what you really want more than being forced into it. Don't be afraid to quit your job or your current business, even if there are a million reasons (aka excuses) to put it off until next month. Each day you do that, you lose another day of your ideal life.

Also, don't have an attractive back-up plan. As Seth Godin states, if you have a back-up plan, you'll always defer to it. So simply focus on the outcome you want, not the alternatives (which may look far more appealing, like real income and job security).

From broke to $15,000 in one month

So there I was. I had a blog that was only read by my Mum and two friends, and a strong desire to work for myself. I also had very little money to my name, so I managed to set up my new Canadian company for under $100.

The next six months were the toughest – and most formative — of my life. I went without any income and on two occasions could barely pay my rent. I was terrified.

When a friend came to visit from New Zealand, I broke down in tears. I was so relieved to see someone who understood me and what I was going through.

My friend believed in me. He'd seen me progress up through the ranks of my corporate career and had witnessed my persistence and dedication to training for the body sculpting competition. I needed someone to have faith in me at this tough time, as I wasn't sure I had enough in myself..

Around this time my parents invited me to fly home and live with them, or to consider getting a job again. The mere mention of that second option made me more determined than ever to make a real go of building my business.

Then, one day, a friend in Vancouver threw me a lifeline. She'd seen what I'd achieved in the time I'd lived there and gave me some social media work for one of her clients.

They were a Groupon-like startup that needed a social media strategist. We had several meetings to discuss how my experience in building FundRazr using social media would help them build their platform.

I'd sent them a proposal for $2,000. I'd never charged that much in my life, but I aimed high for two reasons. One reason was that I've always enjoyed the process of negotiation and was adept at punching way above my weight back in the corporate world; the second was that I only had $18 left in my bank account. There was no way I couldn't win this opportunity.

Lesson 4: *Know your worth*

One thing you have to get a handle on when starting any business is charging what you're worth; based on the value you deliver to your client. This is one of the most challenging areas for entrepreneurs, especially when they're starting out and in need of money. But trust me, if you start off lowballing your prices, it become very hard to raise them. You also have to factor in your own overheads, admin and running costs.

In my third meeting with my potential clients, I decided it was crunch time. I had to clinch the deal by restating why I was exactly what they were looking for. They agreed.

They wrote me a check for 50% upfront and I ran across the road to bank it right after we shook hands. My rent was paid, and I could sleep another night with a roof over my head.

Despite this small win, things didn't get immediately better. I was still worried I'd have to give in and get a job. There was nothing consistent about my revenue and I had no idea about my long-term plan.

Yet I had learned something invaluable for the first time in my life – I could charge people for my existing knowledge.

I could monetize ME.

So I pushed through that tough period, with several sleepless nights, and instead of giving in I relied heavily upon my growing reputation in Vancouver as a social media "expert" – which simply meant I knew just enough more than others to charge for it.

Lesson 5: Find your sweet spot

People tell me all the time that they don't feel good enough at something to make a business out of it, that they're not expert enough, and they have no real skill-set that they can monetize. It's a load of crap.

Everyone on this earth has a sweet spot – the intersection between what you're good (or great) at, what you enjoy – or better yet — love doing, and what people will pay you for. This doesn't mean you have to be an expert. You just need to know a little more than the person who needs, and is willing to pay for, your help.

Next I decided to host a Social Media Bootcamp workshop. I tapped heavily into my existing networks and to my surprise, I managed to sellout not one, but three workshops in a row!

I charged $1500 for a two-day course and made over $15,000 in less than a month!

So what did I do once I'd established myself in this industry? I promptly left town.

I left everything I'd built up in Vancouver to live in Argentina for five months.

Once again my friends thought I was nuts.

But the thing is, like many world travellers, I have trouble staying in one place. Once I feel I've established myself somewhere, once I've made the right contacts, experienced the culture and feel like a local, I tend to want to move on to the next adventure.

After a two-month stint in Los Angeles, staying rent-free at my friends' grand house in Manhattan Beach (it helps to have true friends in high places), I was flying to Buenos Aires and the land of empanadas and tango.

Here's the thing though, I did capitalize on what I'd learned by turning the content from those three workshops into my first-ever digital online program, which launched in November 2010.

I did as much active learning as possible to come up to speed with how to launch a product online, including marketing, membership sites, sales pages, launch sequences and webinars.

Despite losing my voice and being just able to speak on my first-ever webinar, I managed to make one sale of $297 with the 30 people who attended live, and several more after.

Looking back that was a lousy result, but in my mind I'd officially done it. I'd launched a product that people actually wanted to buy, and had made my first few thousand dollars online. That was all I needed to prove to myself that I could turn my *own thing* into a business.

Lesson 6: *Maximize what you've got and never stop testing*

It's crucial that you maximize your existing capital and repurpose what you've already got to create further profits. Be resourceful and hustle. Take what you're already doing and turn it into a number of spin-off products or services. You're a writer? Great! What about writing guides for wannabe writers and selling them on Amazon? Or holding in-person writing workshops, recording those, and packaging those audios into an online self-study course?

The Suitcase Entrepreneur is born

One fine evening in 2010, in a hotel in Las Vegas, The Suitcase Entrepreneur brand was born. I'd been at a conference where I'd spent the entire day answering the same questions:

What's your name? What do you do? Where do you live?

Naturally people were fascinated that I lived nowhere. A few people labeled me the "traveling entrepreneur" until Matthew Goldberg, now a good friend, said "*Oh so you're a kind of Suitcase Entrepreneur.*"

My face lit up, and I knew he was bang on. That's exactly what I was and he suggested I go and buy the domain name straight away.

Once I had that name, my brand was born and I was able to get clear on what I was doing, whom I was helping and what I could offer.

I wrote my best selling **BYOB Build Your Online Business** guide after getting a great response for writing a blog series about building a business online. I updated my social media program and re-launched it.

What's more, I created and launched a high-end mastermind and coaching program for women entrepreneurs with Natalie "*She Takes on the World*" MacNeil.

After our first US$40,000 launch (more than the entire year's salary I made in my first ever job), we knew we were onto something, and this was the audience we wanted to help the most.

During this period I'd become a contributing author for *Forbes* when they picked up an article they liked on my own blog. I also wrote several guest posts for huge authority sites (those that get a lot of traffic and people linking to them), and was appointed as a Nike *Make Yourself Movement* ambassador, as well as having my blog posts syndicated directly on Visa Business Network's site.

I started offering coaching on my site in 2011 and doubled my prices in the first few months when I realized there was more demand – and it was harder work – than I thought. I took on my own coach in 2012 to continue to improve on the momentum I was gaining. All of this resulted in my first 6-figure year in business.

That is just a taste of how the journey of this Suitcase Entrepreneur business started. Let's round this out with the adventure and travel side of life to show you the full picture.

Profile of a digital nomad

To paint a picture of what living the nomadic lifestyle is like, take a look at some examples from my own life. I have:

- Been declared a fiscal nomad and am proud to be a resident in three countries, own two passports and have three international bank accounts

- Travelled to 61 countries on 5 continents to date, and many of those several times over

- Acquired mobile SIM cards from US, NZ, Namibia, UK, Malaysia, Kenya, Canada, Germany and South Africa and counting

- Spent close to 7 full months of my life in airports and getting to and from whichever destination I'm off to next

- Done my best work on these modes of transport – especially offline, and written a book (hey! You're reading it) on planes, trains and boats

- Taken a 54 hour trip – door to door from Wellington to Madrid (I can't sleep on planes)

- Made money in my sleep through selling digital products and programs that are available 24/7

- Coached clients while sitting on a beach, in an airport and in a small Slovakian village in the mountains.

The adventurous claims to fame

Life is meant to be an adventure. Remember: you have all the time in the world to grow up. I have no intention of growing up, but until such a time that I have to, I've done things like this:

Crossed the Myanmar border illegally by mistake, and got chased out by locals with rifles;

Tried to joke around with a security guard in Sydney airport saying I had explosives strapped to my chest … don't ask, silly idea;

Cycled 6,500 km (4,000 miles) from Nairobi, Kenya to Cape Town, South Africa in 2012, raising over $12,500 for charity;

Won a gold medal in Ultimate Frisbee at the 2007 World Beach Championships in Brazil, and played at World Championship level on four different continents since 2006;

Broken a world record for dragon-boating across the English Channel in 2007 with, amongst others, Kate Middleton, the future Queen of England;

Completed a year long experiment in 2004 to get really lean (10% body fat), eating lots of chicken and broccoli and working out 7 days a week, to win a body-sculpting competition, and then competing in NZ Nationals.

Along with travel, adventure makes you well-rounded and ready to face most of the challenges that life throws at you. All of this makes you a better business person as well, because being an entrepreneur is one of the wildest rollercoaster rides you'll ever experience. There are many more adventures detailed in this book for you to learn from too. Got your passport ready?

Get your passport to freedom stamped:

- Write or record an honest conversation with yourself, or a good friend, about what you really enjoy doing, what you're naturally good at and what people you could help today by combining those things into an offering. Brainstorm as many avenues as you can in 20 minutes.

- Work out (with a trusted friend or mentor) whether these are in fact logical and feasible, and rank which ones you'd prefer to do in order of priority.

Chapter 2

The only four things you need to be free.

Freedom is one of those words that can mean different things to different people. It's important to be clear on what it looks like to you in your life, and all the stories and beliefs that prevent you from having it. For me, freedom means always being at choice in my life. I don't do anything that I don't want to do.

~ LEO BABAUTA

Let me ask you a question. If you could be anywhere right now, doing anything you want, where would you be? And what would you be doing?

So my next question is: 'What's stopping you from doing that *right now*?'

I love speaking about how to run your business from anywhere, and people are always surprised at how simple it is to achieve.

The fact is, that the only real thing standing in your way of a life of freedom and adventure is … you.

In this chapter I will seek to show you:

- How to reclaim your childhood dreams and act now

- The four key tools you need to get started

- Why your mindset is of the most importance to your freedom.

Reclaim your childhood dreams

Do you know what you really want to do with your life?

If yes, and it's not what you're doing today, then it's time for a pep talk.

Too many people I meet talk about their dreams for the future, but relegate them to "fantasy" projects. They put up with an unhappy "today" for the scant promise of a better tomorrow.

If that's you, you need to stop this way of thinking. If you're not happy, change it. Start living your ideal lifestyle one step at a time.

You see, it's that easy. It starts with you deciding that you want more out of life than you currently have. Then you can put the pieces together and start building the life you have always wanted.

If you don't believe me, let me tell you about a video that had a profound effect on me and made me commit to live my life the way I do now.

If you've not yet watched Randy Pausch's Last Lecture, then you must. As a professor at Pittsburgh's Carnegie Mellon University, he chose to say good-bye to his family, students and colleagues in a way that will be remembered forever.

Dying of pancreatic cancer, he showed his love of life through this lecture, which has since been watched by millions.

The key message of his *Achieving Your Childhood Dreams* lecture is that you must lead the life you want to lead; the life you dreamed about when you were a kid.

When you're a kid, you're not burdened by the constraints or reality, you're free from adult sensibility and you're free from the received wisdom that stifles creativity and action.

That's what you have to go back to. You have to remember how that feels and take a good hard look at where you are now. If you see a disconnect, then it's time to take action and change.

While I'm not suggesting you do the exact same thing your five-year old self wanted to do, you should develop the mindset that "anything is possible" and you are more than capable of achieving it.

My other key takeaway from that lecture is this:

"Brick walls are there for a reason. They let you prove how badly you want something."

They are there to test your dedication to creating a business and a life you love, which is never going to be easy, but is absolutely worth it.

So how badly do you want a lifestyle of freedom and a business that you love?

The only four things you need

In reality there are just four things you need to build a business and lifestyle from anywhere.

1. Laptop or smartphone

2. Internet connection

3. A sound business idea

4. The right mindset.

When I get people to guess at the answers to this question, the first two are usually easy. They may figure out the third, but it's the fourth one that is really the key to it all – and usually overlooked.

1. Your laptop

Think of this as your new portable office. Every single thing you could possibly need to do to create, connect and communicate can be done at the touch of a button. Software programs, folders and online tools will turn your laptop into the ultimate virtual business wrapped up in a case that weighs less than a 1kg.

Imagine that. It's quite unbelievable to think that you can just slip your entire business into a bag and go anywhere. But in a few short years this will be the norm, and new and better devices will make laptops look like a thing of the past.

You want to be selective about your portable office. You'll want the lightest laptop you can get your hands on. Find one that takes up minimal room, but is still powerful enough to do the work you need it to.

Other factors to consider are battery life, durability, multiple USB ports, serviceability, and compatibility with your other digital devices like smart-phones, electronic readers, cameras and online applications and software.

It also needs to fit your personal preferences and be within your budget. Here are my two suggestions to keep it simple:

MacBook Air: After years of being a PC girl, I made the switch to Apple's **MacBook Air 11"** in 2012 and love it.

It's seriously light (just over 1kg) and takes up no space in my suitcase or carry-on. Admittedly it's a little pricier than many other models, but it was one of the most important investments I made.

The battery life is better than my old PC but maxes out at around 5-6 hours. 128GB is not enough memory so I have an external hard-drive for photos and back up everything else directly to Dropbox.

I also have an iPhone, which acts as my mini laptop, personal videographer and camera. I can synchronize everything I need to between the two, from files to music and podcasts. The Samsung Galaxy is an equally fine choice of smartphone. I think these are the perfect tools for travelers.

The other laptop I would recommend is:

Asus Zenbook UX21: This is an Ultrabook and ranks just behind the Mac-Book Air in terms of value for money. The **Asus Zenbook** is slim (17mm at the thickest point at the back and tapering down to 3mm at the front, as slim as my MacBook Air).

It's light (1.1kg), good looking, has 6GB of ram, and also offers fantastic performance for a very reasonable price – a few hundred dollars less than the MacBook Air.

The USB port uses technology that apparently charges your devices much faster than usual. Running out of juice is a perennial problem for travelers. This is, therefore, a boost.

2. Internet connection

This is something that's only going to become more readily available, which is good news, because it can make or break your day.

There's nothing more frustrating than not being able to connect to the rest of the world when you need it most. The best piece of advice I can give here is to be prepared for not having Internet at any given time.

I talk about this extensively in Chapter 13, including the fastest Internet connections in the world. In short, if you aren't able to access free Wi-Fi in a café or via a direct Ethernet connection, then you can tether to your data plan on your mobile if you have it, buy a Wi-Fi dongle with data on it, or try a private VPN network like Private Wi-Fi.

3. A sound business idea

Knowing what type of business you want to create to fit your ideal lifestyle is simply a matter of knowing what you want your life to look like.

You need to consider factors that include what 'work' looks like to you, how many hours you want to work, whether you want it to be entirely virtual or whether you prefer to work with people face-to-face.

Naturally there are types of businesses that are better suited to being run from a laptop and Internet connection and I cover these in much more detail in Chapter 5.

What you really need to get started in business for yourself is a talent or skill that you can earn money from while on the road. There are numerous avenues to do this, such as freelancing jobs or packaging your skills and talent into products and services.

These can be physical or digital products. Your services can be consulting, coaching, teaching, personal training, design, development, writing, public relations, personal development, finance and so on.

All of this has to be tied in to offering a solution to a problem or challenge that someone has and is willing to pay you for. That is, after all, the basic foundation for starting any business.

The biggest problem I see people face is coming up with an idea, or choosing just one of their many ideas and running with it.

> **The ideas theory**
>
> People are addicted to ideas. Ideas are easy, tantalizing, and always there to play with. Nothing can go wrong with an idea in your head. The real world though, that's messy and you have to (gasp) actually do some work rather than just dream! A pretty threatening thought for a long term ideas addict...
>
> ~ *Marianne Cantwell, founder of Free Range Humans*

4. The right mindset

The right mindset can take you everywhere and anywhere. The trouble is, people have a hard time letting go of what they 'should' be doing, based on what society dictates.

In general, society thinks you should have the fancy office, the house, the car and the mortgage and payments to go along with these things. You should spend all your time working your ass off to earn money so that you can spend it on getting more things.

The truth is, we don't need to live in a material world. Sorry Madonna, we just don't.

The burden of being weighed down by the debt you've incurred from buying the material possessions you really don't need is a heavy one and something you can do without.

There is a reason we have a worldwide financial crisis and an associated increase in the rate of stress-related health problems – the majority of us in the West are living well beyond our means.

The solution? Own less crap. Having a minimalist outlook on life is one of the most freeing things ever and it's great for your wallet.

I am more interested in buying experiences than stuff. I believe you should be too. You really don't need much at all – just your health, a smile and a sense of adventure.

Becoming Minimalist

"After a conversation with my neighbor on Memorial Day 2008, my family and I decided to become minimalist and intentionally live with fewer possessions. We immediately cleared the clutter from our home and life. As a result, we found a valuable new way to life, centered on our most important values. It has been a journey of discovering that abundant life is actually found in owning less. And it still ranks as one of the best decisions we've ever made with our life."

~ Joshua Becker, excerpt from Becoming Minimalist

What's more, there's proof that the minimalist way of living increases your happiness and I cover this in more depth in Chapter 12, as well as examples of people who can back this statement up with how they've transformed their lives for the better.

Having the right mindset goes beyond freeing yourself from your physical possessions and creating space in your everyday life. It's also about getting rid of that excess baggage you're potentially paying a high price for right now; the emotional and intellectual baggage you've been carrying around with you, ever since society went ahead and told you what sort of a normal life you should be leading: one constrained by all the conventional ideas about what's possible.

That baggage is best left at the check-in counter so you can avoid the hefty fees you'll have to pay if you keep it in your possession.

It's all about developing the freedom based mindset

You see, living a life where freedom reigns supreme, where a laptop and internet connection is all you need, is something most people just can't get their head around.

It's a beautiful thing when you do, as you suddenly see the world as your oyster, and the limitations you had in the past giving way to infinite possibilities facilitated by technology, a virtual workforce and affordable travel.

The only trouble is, along with living a different kind of life to everyone else now, you also have to handle their reaction to it. That isn't always easy, especially when you look like the misfit, nomad or rebel.

When I tell people what I do, the most common response is *"Oh Natalie, I'd love to be doing what you're doing"*, to which my response is *"Then why don't you? Let's make it happen"*.

You just need to make the decision to pack up your old life, get rid of your stuff, and if you want to, go traveling. It's that simple, yet people make it so complicated.

Choose freedom

"I woke up one day a few years ago and realized that I could do whatever I wanted with my time. My time was MINE. I could spend it, invest it, or waste it away on frivolities. No one was there to tell me otherwise. Freedom."

~ *Colin Wright, excerpt from Start a Freedom Business*

Yet most people don't think like Colin or you and me. They say they want to live our kind of lifestyle, but they get bogged down in the "realities of life" that they have been fed ever since they dropped their childhood dreams.

They want to create a better life, but they're too scared or too comfortable in their current one.

That's what I want to change with this book. It starts here. It starts with you. It's time to be a kid again and look at possibilities and turning those into realities.

Your mission

- Watch Randy Pausch's Last Lecture and then think back to when you were a kid. Write down all the things you dreamed of doing or being as a kid (that you can remember) and write them in your new notebook.

- Pick the top 3 on that childhood list that you would most like to do and set yourself a goal of achieving them within the next 12 months.

- Look at this list once again and ask yourself, honestly, whether what you're doing right now is what you dreamed of as a kid. If you see a disconnect write down what you're going to do to change it – even if just one idea comes to mind right now. Keep this list (in your new notebook) beside you, and add to it daily.

- Ask yourself where your tolerance level for minimalism lies. What are you actually willing to give up and get rid of, what does "minimal" look like to you? How long and what will it take for you to achieve your desired level?

- If you are having a hard time letting go of "stuff" in your life then read these articles or grab a copy of Man vs Debt's "Sell Your Crap" at **manvsdebt.com/sell-your-crap/** and feel the release!

- Check which of the four things you need to be free are already within your reach and how you can obtain the remaining ones.

Chapter 3

Real stories of others living life on their own terms.

*You can lead a contented life without taking risks, but you'll be
unlikely to live a truly, wildly happy one if you don't*
~ COLIN WRIGHT

Every week I get emails from people who want to live life on their own terms but don't know where to start. These people are desperate to quit their nine-to-five jobs, but have a gnawing feeling of being stuck. I speak to entrepreneurs and freelancers who want to make their current businesses a virtual one, but they're overwhelmed.

I ask everybody who signs up to my Highflyer newsletter to *'hit reply and tell me about yourself'* and when they do, their stories are revealing and valuable. They help me better understand what freedom in business and adventure in life looks like to other people, and they show me how to help them tackle their challenges.

This is one example, from Annaliese Landa:

"I aspire one day to having the freedom to work anywhere in the world – just like you, in fact! And sooner, rather than later! I also want to succeed for others ... so that I can eventually be a source of inspiration and encouragement to anyone who finds themselves on the receiving end of redundancy — to show them that it's not the end, but a new beginning. I was born to write and therein lies my true vocation. To give myself the freedom to follow this path, I plan to investigate as many ways of home-working as possible."

Or this email from Susan Whitehead:

"Our family of seven sold off everything to pursue our dreams of living overseas to lead a life like yours. We moved to Costa Rica on August 7th, 2011 and then spent thirteen months living in Mexico! We had a business we turned over to contractors, about two weeks prior to departure. My husband does marketing consulting for local businesses and is an aviation English consultant and I have a few small income streams with digital products including an iPad magazine, Real Family Travel."

Then I get replies from people who are standing on the precipice of life. They want to take that leap into the world of entrepreneurship and designing their own lifestyle, but they are stuck in the conventional world, either through their own choice, or because of circumstances they feel bound by.

They send messages like this one from Cotey Bucket:

"I grew up traveling {run away train hopper} and have struggled all my life with any attempts to live within the confines of the civilized paradigm most folks find to be so comforting. That's why the idea of the location independent entrepreneur is more than a little appealing to me. Although in all honesty I don't have anything going right now I'm doing my best to funnel my free time into a blogging practice that will at least help me to live the dreams I have for myself.

Right now I suppose it's a bit of a life deferment program in that I plan to work at my current job for the next five years or so in an effort to pay off the loans for a degree I decided half way through that I didn't need, while at the same time developing something of a safety net.

Currently I have a 365 site I'm working on in an effort to up my photography and writing skills {a photo and some words} and hopefully build some accountability and social proof in the process. While working on that I'm also putting together {still in planning phase} my life style {no idea how to label it at this point really} blog and an accompanying free book."

Cotey simply needs to make a choice. He needs to choose freedom and once he commits to that, the rest will work itself out.

If you're shaking your head in disbelief, then know that every single day, people around the world are leaving their conventional reality behind, in order to see what's truly possible.

If you want to join them, it doesn't need to happen "overnight". It can take months, even years to get really clear on what you want, but the journey of discovery is the best part of this adventure.

Simply commit to taking the leap and start living life on your own terms. To show you how, I've included examples of people who have made this important decision for themselves and are now living the life they have always dreamed of, or are working towards achieving that, each and *every* day.

By the way, if you're thinking "Natalie, that's all fine and dandy for a single person with no kids or partner to think about" then I have examples of these people for you too. From singles to couples, families with lots of kids, dogs and horses, single parents, adventurers and philanthropists – you name it. I've got you covered. It's time to drop the excuses and take action.

Let's dive in!

The location independent rebel

In 2009 Sean Ogle was extremely unhappy with his life. He'd been working as a financial analyst and had finally decided that enough was enough. He left his job, moved to Bangkok and spent the next seven months traveling, learning Internet marketing and figuring out how to make his newly-discovered lifestyle more permanent.

"Over the course of the next year, I realized that building a business you can run from anywhere is much simpler than most people think, you just have to complete the steps.

"First, build online skills. I learned search engine optimization, the basics of Wordpress, and copywriting among others. No matter who you are, if you're a solopreneur online, these are the traits that are going to allow you to build the foundation for your business.

"Second, take one of those skills and freelance them. After I had the basics down, I started doing SEO work on a freelance basis. This gave me confidence to know I could support myself, find clients, and make the lifestyle more permanent.

"Finally, when you have the skills, the confidence, and the base of income, you can begin working on your own projects. This could be an information product, affiliate niche site, e-commerce store or any number of other ventures.

"For me personally, it's been a combination of all of the above. My blog Location 180, drives traffic and leads to my other ventures, like my community for entrepreneurs, Location Rebel, or my golf affiliate site Breaking Eighty.

"Bottom line, now I'm able to work whenever I want, from wherever I want, and it's all because I followed those three steps: Build skills, freelance, apply to my own projects."

The food loving travel blogger

In 2008, having long wanted to travel the world, Jodi Ettenburg had saved enough money from working as a lawyer to go on an adventure for a year or two before returning to her normal life. She had been to law school in Canada, where the tuition fees are extremely low by American standards, and she had been able to pay off her debt and put aside some savings during her five years of work as an New York attorney.

"After I left and started my blog Legal Nomads, I thought I would travel for a year then return to New York and work as a lawyer again. Unexpectedly, the site took off and I began to receive freelance work and also realized that I really loved to write and share my experiences in the hopes that others would want to see the world too. And thus began the very organic shift from lawyer to travel writer and more.

"Over the years, I've switched from Blogger to Wordpress, and expanded my business from travel writing to also include photography and curation, as well as partnerships with travel companies I use and respect.

"My focus on the history of food and using what we eat as a tool for learning also led to my first book, **The Food Traveler's Handbook**. This unexpected new career is a work in progress (aren't we all?), but one I am very thankful for.

"I may or may not one day return to the law, for the moment I am happy to continue seeing the world and eating my way through it."

The freedom based business

At 19, Colin Wright quit three of his five jobs and started up his first business: a magazine. Initially successful and then horribly (and quite publicly) failing, Colin learned three very important things from his experience.

He learned that if you're going to start a business, it's probably best to know something about running a business. He learned that, after working at a handful of jobs and starting a magazine, while studying for a dual-emphasis university degree, that failure is just one step on the way to success.

Years later, Colin was running a flourishing branding studio in Los Angeles when he decided to change course again and try something new. He got rid of everything that wouldn't fit into a carry-on bag and hit the road. Colin has been traveling the world ever since, living in a new country every four months, based on the votes of his blog readers.

"Currently my attention is focused on the publishing industry as a whole, from the perspective of an author and that of a businessperson. To date I've written 11 books, hundreds of posts on my blog, Exile Lifestyle, countless missives from the road through a subscription-funded project called Exiles, and co-founded a non-traditional publishing company called Asymmetrical Press.

"Travel and extreme lifestyle experimentation continue to be an important part of my life, as it provides inspiration for my written work, while also giving me the chance to push my own philosophical and experiential boundaries."

Colin tries to hold still every once in a while, but it never lasts very long; trying new things and meeting new people are too much of a draw for him.

The tropical MBA and e-commerce master

Dan Andrews studied Philosophy in college and briefly considered being a musician or a professor, but he realized that he wasn't particularly good at either, nor was he willing to do the work.

So instead he set about learning about e-commerce, which led to a $1 million dollar product-based business that he runs while traveling the globe and living in Bali, the Philippines, Vietnam and Thailand.

"My primary motivation was personal freedom, and when I looked around I saw that people in business seemed to control their destiny more than any other profession. So I moved to California (mostly for the sunshine) and started working my tail off in business roles, focusing mainly on manufacturing products in China.

"After four years of working hard for others I started my own product business with two partners. We founded the business by manufacturing modern cat furniture. That business has since expanded into other product lines, including portable bars. We employ 13 people worldwide, and bring in over $1 million in revenue each year.

"In 2009, I started a publishing company with my friend Ian. We produce the Lifestyle Business Podcast (consistently ranking in iTunes Top 25 Business Podcast), the online community Dynamite Circle, with over 500 of the web's most prominent location independent entrepreneurs, and we also provide SEO services.

"I believe business and lifestyle should mix, and you should simply enjoy yourself. I feel privileged to be in a position that allows me to appreciate seeing the world and work with like-minded entrepreneurs doing the same thing."

The digital marketing consultant

Daryl Mander slaved away for 8 years building a career in digital marketing agencies in London, UK. He started saving money for a year-long travelling adventure as he badly needed a break from the repetitive, mind numbing, stressful London life.

He got to the point where he was ready to pull the trigger, quit the job and just leave for a year. Then he read Tim Feriss's book, *The 4-Hour Workweek*, and it changed his perspective.

"I realized that with the money I had saved, I could either blow it on a year long travel fest, or I could invest it in my own business and work towards creating a life of freedom. I chose the second option.

"In August 2012, I left my job. I sold everything I owned, I rented out my apartment, packed a bag and moved to Malaysia. I had no income, but I had enough savings to fund me until I found an income stream.

"Less than one year later and I am earning more as a self-employed, location-independent, digital marketing consultant than I was in my 8 year long advertising agency career. I help clients to make more sales by advertising online and ranking highly in search engines.

"I work anywhere from 20-30 hours per week for my clients, and the best part is I get to choose when and where I do my work for them. I've lived in Malaysia and Vietnam, have spent a lot of time in Singapore, and Thailand and Japan are big on my hit list of places to visit now that I have 'found my freedom.'"

The new age lifestylers

Leanne Pittsford and Leah Neaderthal are the co-founders of **Start Somewhere**, where they use design and technology to make companies look great online. They work with nonprofits, social enterprises and small businesses with a social mission, (and they also redesigned my website back in July 2012!)

They're a couple who work and travel with each other and their two dogs. With San Francisco as their "home base", they choose a few international places each year in which to spend a few months, live like locals, and really experience the city. So far they've spent extended stays in Buenos Aires and Berlin, as well as various cities in Southeast Asia.

"We started the business while we were on a year-long trip around the world. We had been backpacking, but about 2 months in, we realized a few things:

1) We love to work and regardless of where we were in the world, we'd continue to think about new business ideas and ways to make them happen;

2) Instead of backpacking and moving quickly through each place, we preferred staying in cities for a longer period of time.

3) After working for ourselves, there's no way we could go back to full time desk jobs!

"So, we decided to change the plan and focus our energies into the business so we could make it a lifestyle, and not a year long time-out from "normal life." That's how Start Somewhere and our life as location independent entrepreneurs were born."

The full tilt single Mom

Single mum Rebekah Tyler decided there was more to life than working hard as a part-time teacher to support her kids.

Orphaned from the age of four, Rebekah Tyler was brought up by her beloved grandmother, and was devastated when she died in 2007. Already struggling with raising her two sons on her own, Rebekah had reached breaking point.

With nothing left to lose, she knew things had to change.

Four months later, Rebekah sold her house, quit her job and took her two sons, aged 2 and 10, on an eight-month adventure around the world, travelling to Canada, England, France, Spain, Italy and Vietnam.

Following her return to New Zealand, she threw herself into writing a novel called *Full Tilt*.

"When I returned to New Zealand I felt lost and somewhat disenchanted with being back in my home town where everything felt the same. So I threw myself into writing my novel, *Full Tilt*, to share my journey and inspire others who may feel trapped with their lives to make a change.

"The writing journey led to many wonderful experiences, meeting new people and learning new skills, which gave me a sense of purpose and meaning to my life like never before."

Staying true to her independent spirit, she decided to publish the book herself and launched a crowd-funding campaign on Kickstarter in 2013, reaching her goal of $10,000 just half way in.

Rebekah believes that you can achieve anything in life and that you do not have to settle for the mundane daily grind. As long as you have determination and perseverance anything is possible, hence her 2nd goal: to have a

New York Times Bestseller!

The globetrotting family

Rachel Denning had never traveled outside the United States until she was married with four children. She took a trip with her husband Greg that ignited a flame for more adventure.

Together, Greg and Rachel discovered that 'the world is too big to stay in one place', and that they wanted to *live deliberately*, to 'suck the marrow out of life', as Thoreau says.

Wanting her children to experience other cultures and customs, to learn languages and to have the world as their classroom, she and Greg moved their family — four children under age four — to Costa Rica in 2007 (which began with an epic road trip from the U.S.)

Since that time, they've pursued long-term family travel, living in the Dominican Republic, India, Georgia, Alaska and Guatemala (and visiting 12 countries in all.)

"Living the life you *really* want to live *is* within your power. You simply have to believe in yourself, and take consistent action toward turning that dream into reality (or putting foundations under those castles in the sky.)"

They've passionately sought the answer to 'how to fund travel', and discovered first hand — and from the people they've met along the way — that it is possible.

Greg and Rachel earn what they call a 'patchwork' income: cash flow that comes from multiple sources, such as advertising on their websites, like their blog, Discover Share Inspire, affiliate sales, freelance writing, personal coaching, mentoring and network marketing.

Having never traveled much before having children, their naiveté gave

Greg and Rachel a 'can do' attitude about traveling with four small kids (they had a fifth in 2010!)

"Traveling with your family is not only doable, it's like a MasterCard commercial ... priceless. You'll never regret making the decision (and effort) to do it. Ultimately, family travel requires that you become the best parent you can. The better your parenting skills, the easier traveling with children becomes. And the more you travel, the more adaptable your kids become -- it gets easier as you go!"

The flexpat home exchangers

Hannah and Chris Alford wanted to be able to work from wherever they liked and explore the world as much as possible.

To make that happen, they've focused on making money from more than one source. They juggle lots of different business areas, which keeps it interesting, and doesn't leave them too vulnerable to market changes.

"We set our business up so it supports our lifestyle — not the other way round. The most 'traditional' of our businesses is an HR consultancy. We can manage a lot of the work for this from overseas, but also need to be in the UK for some months of the year to meet with clients or to deliver some projects in person.

"Because we choose to live in our UK home for a few months a year anyway, this fits in perfectly. Having a base in the UK means we can home exchange and live in other countries rent-free. If this doesn't work out off-peak villa rentals are another convenient option.

"In addition to this we have two e-commerce stores where we sell study guides and professional coaching services to niche markets; much of this business is very automated, although it took a few years to get to that stage.

"We also have our Love Play Work website where we write about our travel and business adventures, and recently launched a luxury and boutique hotel review site. These parts of the business open up all sorts of opportunities for us to take exciting trips and then share it with our audience. These parts of the business open up all sorts of opportunities for us to take exciting trips and then share it with our audience."

The full time adventurer

For UK-born adventurer **Dave Cornthwaite**, the quarter-life crisis kicked in at age 25. He had a stale three-year relationship, a mortgage, a cat and a well-paid but painful job.

"I loved the cat, the rest was destroying me. All around me there were folks living miserable lives and not doing themselves justice, and the sad thing was I could see myself being exactly like them because it was easier to carry on living the life I'd made for myself. Easier, but way more depressing than something else.

"Ultimately, I decided I wanted to respect the answer when somebody asked me what I did for a living. As soon as I decided that, I opened up to new possibilities. Eventually one showed up, a skateboard. Not the usual catalyst to encourage someone to quit their job but that's exactly what happened.

"After two weeks of skating, the town I'd lived in for six years looked like a different place. So I skated to work, left the keys on the desk, and skated out with two promises: One, I was never going to work for anyone else. Two, I wanted to skate further than anyone else ever had. Ever.

"So I did it. 4500 miles in 8 months, along with two world records and one book deal. That was 2006. Ever since life has become more unconventional by the month, but it's my convention, it's normal to me.

"I sold my house and moved onto a boat. Tried and failed at a couple of businesses but always went back to adventure. Money started to come from speaking gigs and book sales. I got my gear free from sponsors after a couple of years, lived simply, spent little, slowly formed my own philosophy and worked hard.

"I've done things that nobody else has done but only because I made a decision to, nothing special. My motivation: doing what I love is the most important thing in my life. Everything becomes possible when you shape your decisions around passion. And even better, I friggin' love Mondays!!"

The natural horse coach

Based in Quebec, Canada, **Geneviève Benoit** helps horse lovers who are committed to building a long-term harmonious partnership with their horse. She's on a mission to guide them to become natural horsemen (or women) and accelerate their learning, both on the ground and in the saddle.

"I actually left a high-paying high-tech career after 20 years in the corporate world to design my dream life coaching natural horsemanship.

"I do a lot of my teaching in person with human and horse, but I also do one-on-one video coaching program to help horse owners around the world advance and to support their learning at a more affordable cost. Students send me a video clip of a play session with their horse, I take a look and we discuss it over Skype. I have students in various parts of Canada, in Europe and as far as Bali and China!

"My next goal is to generate more residual and leveraged income to keep my dream alive by creating an online class format to expand my coaching from one-on-one to reach a greater number of students who can continue advancing without having to travel to a clinic or facility.

"At home, my own horses are boarded at a facility near where I live so if I leave for a few days, the owners of the barn look after them. However, if I am on the road for any length of time, they come with me. I have a horse trailer with a small living quarters section out front where I live on the road — complete with shower, toilet, microwave, propane stove, heat and air conditioning.

"I stop at horse farms or fairgrounds on the way to let the horses out overnight and will often spend several days or weeks in one location where my horses can have a pasture or paddock while I live in my trailer right on the property.

"I carry my laptop, a small printer and basic office fixtures to keep working on the road. As long as I have Wi-Fi, I can keep in touch and plan my next event.

"The horse trailer is my home away from home, it has a tack room, feed room, horse stalls and my little 8 x 10 living space complete. It is a simple life, but I love being able to live where my horses are and to see them from my window when I get up in the morning!

"It is my version of happiness!"

The philanthropic misfits

Five years ago, A.J. decided to stop living somebody else's humdrum, average life and walked away from a 6-figure job as a finance executive in Manhattan.

Since that time, AJ and his wife Melissa launched Misfit Incorporated, a business that is meaningful and allows them the freedom to wander around the world, work together and build a for-profit business that serves as an engine for philanthropy.

They've raised millions of dollars to build schools, bring fresh water and health and sanitation programs to communities in Kenya, Ethiopia, Tanzania, South Sudan and Malawi. They're also on a quest to travel around the entire world, over land and sea (living on every continent) through the next five years.

"Misfit Inc. is made up of six full-time employees and is effectively an umbrella organization that allows us to run a myriad of sub-businesses and projects, the largest of which is Misfit Creative, our services business where we focus on high-end handcrafted web design, engineering and content strategy for VC-backed startups and larger technology companies.

"In addition to Misfit Creative, we run a quarterly magazine, a conference, a subscription program called Honorary Misfits, a web application called Twitgift, and our design and apparel company called Trendy Misfit.

"We launched an annual social philanthropy project, and we use all of our commercial businesses to fund the 20% of our time as a company that we spend on humanitarian and social work.

"However, at the center of everything we do is our ethos to live life with intention and do work that truly matters, which we write about extensively at Pursuit of Everything. This is the true essence of Misfit."

Anything is possible

Now that you've taken the time to read these inspiring real-life examples, you'll want to take some serious action and get started for yourself.

There is no circumstance or situation that you can't make the most of, and nothing holding you back but you, regardless of where you came from and what challenges you're facing.

So go on. I dare you!

How to apply these stories to your life

- Tune into which of these stories resonated with you most and visit their blogs (you'll find links at **suitcaseentrepreneur.com/book/ resources** Chapter 3).

- Take inspiration from their personal journeys to leading their ideal lifestyle and work arrangements to suit their needs and fulfill their dreams.

- Commit to take one action today that sets you on your own path to creating your unique journey.

Act 2

How to build an online business you can take anywhere.

Entrepreneurship is living a few years of your life like most people won't, so that you can spend the rest of your life like most people can't.
~ UNKNOWN

Starting your own business out of sheer passion for what you do, determination and tenacity is certainly admirable, but it needs to be backed up by a business that solves a specific problem or challenge your niche market has.

It also means you have to hustle, which means consistently working on strategic actions that drive your business forward.

Ones that ensure you have a business that lives primarily online and can be packed up at a moment's notice and taken anywhere around the world.

"I once had a job that I had to show up for everyday. Alarm goes off, hit snooze ... once, twice, three times before I'd drag myself out of bed, get in the shower, suit up and make my way into the office through 20 miles of Los Angeles traffic.

"I dreamed of working from home, having more time with my family, total flexibility, the ability to travel, and waking up each morning brimming with the excitement of getting to work on my creative projects.

"Today, that's a reality. Each morning I jump out of bed excited about getting onto my laptop and helping people discover their own path to sovereignty. I am financially liberated, not because I have millions in the bank, but because I know how to earn exactly what I need when I need it.

"As a result, I don't have to worry about saving for retirement or waste my life doing work I hate just so I can pay the bills.

"**It all started with one simple shift.** I got into more truth than I'd ever been before about what I really needed to have the life I wanted. I broke free of the false conditioning and fear patterns keeping me stuck by discovering my Money Map Number and my personal entrepreneurial archetype so I could build an income model in alignment with the truth of who I really am. Now, you can do the same. For free.

Thanks to Alexis Neely for sharing her journey and for being a sponsor of this act.

"Go to **moneymaptofreedom.com/truth** and use coupon code FREETOOL to get a 100% discount on the Money Map Truth-Telling Module."

Chapter 4

The future of work and why there is no better time than now to build your own business.

The best way to predict the future is to create it.
~ PETER DRUCKER

Ten years ago, if somebody had told me:

"Natalie, imagine a world where you can run your company from anywhere, in the cloud, or from that smartphone you're holding in your hand. Imagine that you can hire and manage a team of virtual workers from around the world via video, who you may never meet and who never need to set foot in an office."

I might have replied, "Are you kidding me? That's not possible … and what on earth is a smartphone and how do I get into a cloud?".

Of course, this is now: no imagination necessary. We are living in a new era for small businesses that is beyond exciting.

We have an abundance of information and tools, which are increasingly accessible, cheap and powerful, right at our fingertips, with amazing capabilities. Heck, we even have 3D printers, space tourism, and sunscreen pills.

But what does all this mean for you?

Let's take a look at:

- Eight key trends that are transforming the world we live in

- Where you should be focusing your attention to achieve maximum return

- How to become a leading learner and stay a step ahead of the rest.

The top eight trends defining the future of work

Technology and tools are changing at a rapid pace.

If you are serious about creating a business that will remain relevant and competitive for years to come you can't ignore these trends. But you don't want to waste time following them blindly, either. The trick is knowing which ones you need to make your own vision for your business and life come true.

Here are the key trends affecting us all:

1. Global marketplace gets personal

Thanks to our global markets becoming increasingly interconnected and accessible, entrepreneurs and small businesses will find more opportunities to work and partner together across cultures and locations. This means being able to reach a large percentage of the entire world's population, and all the challenges and opportunities that come along with that.

To take advantage of this you will need to excel at producing specialized products and services to meet the personalization demands of customers. This means catering to your target audience with specific language and location-based features like **Viewsy**, a location analytics solution for the physical stores to better understand their foot traffic.

2. The rise of the entrepreneur

Small businesses are already taking advantage of web and mobile technologies that allow them to take on the corporate giants, with customers no longer knowing, or even caring about the size of the firm that provides their goods and services.

The barriers have been removed, so there's nothing stopping you from setting up an online business in a few hours and for less than $100. You can use WordPress or **LeadPages** to build a landing page for your offer, insert a PayPal button and start selling right away.

Business-to-business services that cater to the growing virtual and global nature of our business world will be at the forefront, like **Mist.io** – a service that allows you to manage and monitor your virtual machines across clouds, using any device that can access the web.

3. Virtual workforces explode

We've already shifted towards a flexible, on-demand workforce that enables businesses of all sizes to get more done with less. This mobile and virtual workforce can scale according to your needs and demands.

It's going to become more common to have a global team that allows you to grow a truly international business. What's more, you can access almost any expertise, with even the tiniest budget, regardless of time-zone or language barrier. Talking of language barriers, **Bableverse** offers an on-demand voice translation service by pro interpreters and bilinguals, in any language and situation.

4. Mobile domination is calling

As technology prices fall, the adoption of sophisticated mobile technologies will continue to permeate our everyday lives. In time, smartphones will replace or bypass desktops and laptops and will emerge as the new standard for both businesses and consumers.

You may well be running your business from a smartphone-like device in just a few years. Given that 1.5 million new Android devices are activated daily, according to **Adrian Kingsley-Hughes,** we may soon see Android-powered PCs.

Along with mobile devices, we're going to become increasingly mobile thanks to wearable technologies like **Google Glass** that bring real time sharing and connection into everything we do, anytime, anywhere. There's no reason to sit behind a laptop any more.

5. Consumers are the new CEOs

From our reliance on (and increasing addiction to) mobiles, and with smartphones becoming smarter, our ability to have real influence as consumers grows. We can make more informed decisions about what we purchase and why.

We're Googling first, on multiple devices, in order to research products like never before. We search for real opinions about a product by checking out sites and forums before we buy online or set foot in a store.

We demand products and services that fit with our digital preferences and mobile lifestyles. Look at **CLYC**, the first digital bicycle lock with an automatic keyless function, making your bicycle a mobile app. No more losing your keys, just connect with your smartphone and you're off pedaling.

6. Social is your business foundation

Social media has transformed the way we market, sell and serve our customers. Platforms like Facebook, YouTube and Google Plus have made this consumer power even more possible.

We trust recommendations from friends and our extended networks influence our purchasing decisions. Yelp and Foursquare check-ins guide our decisions on what to do and see. TripAdvisor reviews inspire many of us on where to eat, sleep and travel – right down to what we order off the menu!

Vitamin Water saw huge success 'way back' in 2010 when they handed over product development to their Facebook fans using their interactive platform the "Vitamin Water Flavor Creator". More than 1 million people participated, leading to a 1000% increase in Facebook fans, the creation of 40,000 virtual bottles and the development of a new product, Vitamin Water's 'Connect', which hit the retail shelves shortly thereafter.

7. Digital currency is king

It's becoming easier and more accessible to do online banking and to make mobile payments. Digital wallets like **Google Wallet** and smartphone apps from major banks are opening the door for us to manage our finances from anywhere and to make payments from anywhere.

As consumers become more trusting, we will find ourselves in an increasingly cashless society, turning to tools like **Trustev**. This is a real-time, online verification for shopping online that uses social fingerprinting technology to create a real and visible relationship between consumer and retailer.

8. Crowdfunding is the new angel investor

You don't need to hit up investors anymore and give away large chunks of control of your company, instead you just need to turn to one of over 500 crowd funding sites to finance your dreams. In fact, it's such an important trend, that I wrote a book on it: **How to Fund Your Dream Idea on Kickstarter.**

While I think this crowd funding movement is limited and will morph significantly in the next few years, it's still a method more of us will embrace to raise funds for our projects, build buzz and create platforms from which to actually launch. It's already spawning a whole new breed of initiatives, products, services and movements.

How to take advantage of these trends

Now that you're aware of future trends that are impacting our lives right now, it's time to look at how you can actually make them relevant to your life and business.

It's great to know that we might live to be 200 years old, but that's of no use if we're not building a sustainable business and lifestyle.

> "It's not about how you work 10 times harder. It's about how you work 10 times smarter and everything to do with how you find a wave that's 10 times bigger. It doesn't matter what kind of business you're in, there's going to be a way for you to leverage waves."
>
> ~ *Roger Hamilton, author of* **Fast Forward Your Business.**

The trick to taking advantage of these "waves" is to pick the ones you can ride most effectively.

Imagine you're a surfer. You want to catch these waves early and then ride them all the way to the beach. But first you need to learn how to catch the wave and get up on the board. So let's start paddling.

Mobilize yourself

Mobile is huge. You're going to have the ability to be in five billion people's pockets in 10 years' time and that's going to impact your business in ways you can't yet imagine.

Right now, there are close to 2 billion people with mobiles and 181 million with smartphones, of **which 75% are Android**, not Apple. For westerners, mobile phones offer a delightful consumer convenience; we can buy, sell, eat and sleep more efficiently thanks to our smartphone.

But there are far more mobile users in Africa than in the U.S. or Europe, and China's mobile growth will be four times as big as the US market alone four years from now. For many people in poorer countries, mobiles are capital equipment.

This means that if you're not prepared to cater to the varying needs of this growing global audience of 2 billion mobile users, you're missing a really huge sales opportunity.

The good news is that, by default, the very tools you're building your business with are all focused on capturing this market too, by embedding mobile friendly features.

How to use mobile in your business

People are going to their favorite places like Facebook and YouTube to search for what they're after, so just by having your presence on these key social media sites you're far more likely to be found.

Luckily for you, each of these social media and e-commerce platforms has mobile friendly versions and features in place to take payments. You can put up a store on Amazon or eBay and straight away you are optimized for mobile. The same applies for your Facebook Page.

Email client managers like Mailchimp and Aweber have mobile friendly templates you can use and if you're building an app you can sell it in the iTunes store or in Google Play.

To really tap into this massive opportunity, I suggest you consider joining the booming app market, which is growing at an unprecedented rate and will **reportedly be worth $25 billion by 2015.**

Want proof for the commercial viability of apps? Domino's Pizza generated over a million dollars in pizza sales every week, within three months of putting out their iPhone app in the US, and within two weeks of releasing their **Android app they had 140,000 downloads.**

Domino's is not a technology company. These guys deliver pizza. The point is, they knew people were already ordering pizzas. They just offered their customers a smarter way to order more – from their mobiles.

Right now I can hear you saying, "Natalie, I'm not really into technology. I know I should be on mobile, but really I don't want to spend a lot of money to have an app designed".

First, ask yourself these questions:

- What do you have of value that you want to put in someone's pocket

- What's the message? What's your content or what's your product?

- How are you implementing a mobile strategy in everything that you do?

Now let me show you some very affordable and easy-to-use tools to get you started. Many weren't around a year ago, but by the time you read this, I can guarantee that there will be many more available for you to choose from.

Key mobile app tools

ShoutEm and **Bizness Apps** are mobile app makers that allow you to create an app without any effort or programming. You simply set up an account, use their platform to create an app step-by-step for almost anything, then hit publish. You pay a monthly fee to host your app.

iBuildApp is a fully functional platform allowing you to create a catalogue, magazine or an iPad app, for which it's been specifically designed. They claim you can do this in 5 minutes and offer a low basic monthly fee. Pay more for premium features.

Newsstand is a service provided by Apple to allow you to easily and simply deliver magazine and newspaper content via free or paid subscription. Apple takes a 30% cut of your subscription fee in return for placing you in front of millions of iStore customers.

Magzter offers a similar service as Newsstand but focuses on foreign titles and the growing base of Android-based tablets. With 7 million readers worldwide, they take a 50% cut of your subscription.

Kindle Publishing allows you to self-publish your blog quickly and easy on the Kindle Store and then allows people to subscribe for free or a fee. It's simple to set up. You just need your RSS feed and to fill in some details. It is a great way to monetize your blog.

The power of video

People are watching more video online than ever before, and we're watching a lot of video on our mobiles, YouTube receives over 600 million views a day and over three billion hours of video are currently watched per month.

"Video on the Web works for you 24 hours a day, introducing you and your services, capturing leads, selling and delivering your products. Your videos never sleep. They are like your virtual workforce and they never ask for a pay rise. That's why I am so excited about the power of video to leverage your time and to create more income around the clock, whatever your business. In short, video sells more!"

~ **Jules Watkins,** *Former MTV and BBC Producer/Director*

More video means more bandwidth. Enter **Google Fiber**. This is an Internet and cable solution, allowing users in some parts of the US to access data 100 times faster than the rest of the world.

Advances like these are useful since consumers continuously require more access to the Internet, watching millions of different channels from portable devices whenever they want. According to analyst Andrew Ladbroke, there will be 800 million smart TVs by 2017!

So you need to be creating video. There's nothing stopping you from creating a professional three-minute video that sells your business and acts as an online brochure for what you do.

Mobile apps like **Vine**, that allows you to shoot short 6 second videos, is working well for brands who've been seeing success with short adverts.

Instagram video allows you to take 15 second videos, which works perfectly for building your brand in short entertaining or educational snippets. No doubt YouTube will continue to innovate to challenge these competitors.

Ask yourself: What is my mobile strategy and what is my video strategy for this next year?

Can your business be presented as an entertainment channel instead of a website?

If you're already blogging, podcasting and publishing videos, what's stopping you from taking it a step further?

How do you change your messaging? How do you change your products? How are you designing for that?

How do you show up in front of people because they want to watch and experience what you're doing?

What is your video marketing strategy for this year and beyond?

Now you might be thinking you're no video expert and you don't have the production skills for doing this, but that doesn't matter. There are plenty of services, products and software to help you do this easily.

And if you hate being on camera, you don't even have to be in your own videos. To create a video for your product or service, you can simply make a PowerPoint presentation, record your screen and talk over the top of it.

Tools to get started with video-tainment

YouTube. Start with a YouTube Channel and 'broadcast yourself'. Not only is this a way to sell yourself and your business, it's an incredibly powerful search engine in itself and it's free.

Animoto is a great tool that takes your photos and videos and turns them into professional videos you can download and embed anywhere. It's very simple to use and has a monthly fee. You don't need any extra software and you can create a video masterpiece complete with music and titles that you can use as your promotional video.

Ezvid allows you to both record your screen and edit the video. It's all done online and it's designed for YouTube. It doesn't get much simpler than this. You can create a PowerPoint or Keynote presentation, talk over the top of it and record your screen to make a training video. It's great for Windows.

Screencast is a great tool for this too and it's good for both MAC and PC.

Top tips for your video marketing strategy

Use the tools above as the basis for what you're going to be producing. Start getting into the habit every week of saying, "Whatever I'm doing in my business, how am I going to record it and share my knowledge with my community?".

Telling your story is critical. It's not just about the benefits and features of your product or service. Talk about the need that you're fulfilling and for whom, so that after three minutes of watching your video people can take action and buy from you.

Create meaningful messages that people want to consume and share. You're competing with 72 hours of video going up every minute. Present your information easily and simply. Engage your audience so that they become part of your story too.

There are thousands of resources and videos available online that you can learn from. To make it easy for you though, I highly recommend you check out both **Gideon Shalwick** and **James Wedmore** for excellent video tips and advice. They're both pros.

Micro and mobile payments

To stay ahead of the competition you have to continually ask yourself how you can deliver more quality, more easily and more cheaply than anyone else. How you can give the most value to your customers?

The beauty of having a virtual, online business is that you can offer value to your customers at a fraction of the cost of businesses who have high overheads. You also get to deliver your products and services that much more quickly via online platforms.

You can even acquire customers for less than $1. Upload a book to Amazon for just $0.99c and sell subscriptions for $1 per month. This is the era of micropayments.

Mobile payment purchases are expected to increase to $1 trillion by 2017, given that we are wandering around with mobiles all the time. Consumers are using their phones like payment processors. If they see something they like, they're buying it in an instant.

Ask yourself: How can I make it even easier for people to buy from me?

Are you using a mobile-friendly shopping cart on your website?

Can people pay you online via several methods like PayPal, Google checkout and credit card?

Do you offer payments in person using your phone when meeting with clients at networking events, trade shows, conferences or in cafés?

Have you set up trial subscriptions of your products or services starting from $1 using PayPal subscriptions for example?

Can you repurpose your current content (blog, podcast, video) into a $0.99c Amazon book to generate new leads or split out a current product or service into smaller bite-size offerings for under $10?

The payments space is developing at a rapid pace as more providers compete for a slice of the market, which means great things for you and me. What's more, many of these tools, services and apps integrate with the existing tools you love to use like your email client, website platform and CRM system.

Key tools to make payments a breeze

PayPal's app lets you send and receive payments from your mobile, plus you get handy notifications when you pay or receive money to your phone. Yet it's still secure so people can't access your account if your phone is stolen. **PayPal Here** has a card reader which plugs into the headset socket, turning your smartphone into a credit card payment processor too.

Square has really led the way on the payments front. You can download their Square Wallet app, link your credit card and then simply say your name to buy things! Like PayPal Here, Square also offers a free card reader which can be attached to your iphone or Android smartphone. They now offer **Square Terminal**, which turns your iPad into a cash register. Square is currently only available in the US, Canada and Japan.

iZettle offers an app to install and a miniature card reader (suitable for both individuals and businesses) for a fee of 2.7% and caters for several European countries. They have also introduced a card reader that accepts chip and pin (check their website for where they're expanding into).

Something to think about....

Imagine if every one of your customers could sell your products for you. They might be talking to a friend about the watch they bought from you that they absolutely love. Their friend likes it too and wants to buy one. They can whip out their mini card-reading device and sell on your behalf, for an affiliate commission, right then and there. You're able to reach thousands more people without doing the marketing or sales, by putting the power in the hands of your fans.

The future of payments

In the last two years a whole new currency has been established called **Bitcoins**. It's a peer-to-peer open-source digital currency and it has created a community-driven eco-payment system.

As a new user, you **choose a wallet** that you will install on your computer or on your mobile phone. Once installed, it generates your Bitcoin address, which you can then share with your friends so they can pay you, or vice versa.

It's works in a similar way to email. Even though it's still in its infancy, it's gaining a lot of popularity, particularly in Europe. The total value of all

Bitcoins in circulation (in April 2013) is already over US $1.3 billion.

Then there's **Ripple** that aims to take payments even further. Ripple acts as a global system for making transactions of any kind, be it US dollars, Euros, Bitcoin, Yen or any other existing currency for virtually free. The future is bright.

Become a leading learner

The pace at which new technology is being developed is quite incredible. Even how we communicate and socialize has changed dramatically since the inception of social media.

If you're prepared to learn a specific skill, like video marketing for nutritionists, or helping Real Estate agents with their copywriting and marketing, you can actually establish yourself as a specialist, or as Roger Hamilton calls it, a Leading Learner.

> "Things are moving so quickly, we want to follow someone who's keeping up with the times. We don't want to follow someone who's relying on his old knowledge. So this is about someone who's forward leading instead of backward leading. A leading learner is not someone who's an expert at knowing. A leading learner is someone who's an expert at doing."
>
> *~ Roger Hamilton*

Taking that one step further and creating your own information-based products and programs to teach others, establishes you as the go-to person in that market. Plus it's a legitimate business model; in fact I'd say it's made for suitcase entrepreneurs (as you'll see in Chapter 5).

Take a look around and you'll see experts like David Siteman Garland who's coined the phrase "Mediapreneurs" after creating a highly successful show Rise To The Top. To date, David has interviewed hundreds of entrepreneurs on his show and podcast.

Thanks to some serious hustle and business smarts he's used his platform to publish a book and makes hundreds of thousands of dollars a year through sponsor agreements. He's gone on to create his own information products and programs teaching you how to do the same like '**Create Awesome Online Courses**'.

Two ways to set yourself apart from the rest

If your brain is already working overtime with ideas on how you can turn what you know into a real business, here are two areas to concentrate on and personally set yourself apart.

As I explain in more detail in Chapter 6, the basic underlying premise is to make yourself incredibly useful and valuable to others who are navigating the seas of change.

1. Simplifying information overload

The average American consumes, on average, 11-12 hours of information a day. As a result, many people are suffering from information overload. The plus side is that services and brands that remove some of that clutter are in increasing demand.

So how about launching a product or app to help simplify someone's life or the daily tasks they undertake?

2. Supplying quality over quantity

Driven by environmental, economic, and social concerns, people want more from everything they buy. This will show not just in *what* they purchase, but also in *how* they purchase. Expect to see more bartering, renting, and swapping.

But this doesn't mean you should be discounting. In fact, you should always look to provide incredible quality in whatever you do, as there's a return in providing boutique services and offerings.

In an age where people can get most 'how-to' information for free online, your strength will come in packaging it in a way that adds value to your customer's life and enriches what they do.

It's like the return of the boutique travel agent who gives superior service to you and customizes your entire holiday, even though you can spend hours yourself researching and booking it all online.

Of course there are a gazillion different ways to capitalize on these trends as they unfold before our very eyes. You don't have to reinvent the wheel, you just have to reinvent yourself and your skills to ensure you stay one step ahead of the rest of the world.

Aim to be an early adopter with a future-focused outlook on life and make time to educate yourself by reading about these emerging trends, before they even happen.

I recommend you follow futurists and big picture thinkers like **Ray Kurzweil** (technology), **Khan Academy** (education), **Virgin Galactic** (space travel), **Oliver Bussmann** (the global workforce) and **Dr. Gene Robinson** (global climate).

How can you tap into the future right now?

- Look at the range of tools featured in this chapter and consider which ones you can use to make things better for your customers right now.

- Ask yourself if you're ready to future-proof your business and be willing to invest in new technology to continually adapt your content and platform?

- Consider what skills you already have, and which of those you can place more effort in learning more on to position yourself as a Leading Learner.

- Check out my YouTube Channel at **youtube.com/nataliesisson** and how I use videos to add value and build my brand, plus download my mobile app on iTunes and Google Play.

Chapter 5

Building an online business for your Suitcase Entrepreneur lifestyle.

The reason you are here is because you've been called. Your real job is to hear what that is and honor it.

~ OPRAH WINFREY

So I assume you want more freedom in your life and the flexibility to work from anywhere? You're not looking to do 80+ hours of work per week, that leaves you stressed out, depressed and without purpose.

You probably want to travel more, for longer, and you're going to need a steady stream of income to fund that lifestyle. You're in the right place.

Deep down, I believe that most of us want to live a life that makes us feel as though we are fulfilling our purpose in life and are making a difference in the world. Personally, I love making a HUGE impact on other entrepreneurs' lives. I want people to love what they do and do it really well.

The good news is that this chapter is going to show you:

• The benefits of building an online business

- How to start a business when you have no idea what to do

- The entry costs and fundamentals of starting an online business

- Four steps to finding your sweet spot

- The only two ways you should make money online

- Six steps to building your online business

The benefits of building an online business

Having your own online business means the freedom to do what you want from anywhere in the world. Online businesses can run 24 hours a day, 7 days a week, and you want to milk that! You, on the other hand, don't have to work those sorts of hours.

You can send one email and make hundreds, or even thousands of dollars. You can launch a new service and make more money in one day than you used to make in one month, or you can package your hard-earned knowledge into an evergreen product that you produce once, but which pays you over months or even years.

This is my life, and the lives of others, too. We have all learned the hard way and we have failed. We have failed a lot; screwing up, running webinars that sucked, making costly mistakes, spending too long on figuring out how to install a plugin on a blog or on creating a 'perfect' sales page. However, we have gone on to create businesses that allow us plenty of flexibility and a lifestyle we love.

The key benefits of this type of business are:

- low start up costs compared to a traditional business or franchise;

- flexibility to set your own schedule and work full or part-time;

- potential for high earning in a relatively short amount of time;

- ability to monetize yourself by selling your knowledge and skills.

What sort of business do you want to own?

"The key difference in starting a Freedom Business over a standard business is a shift in what kind of value it produces for the entrepreneur who starts it (i.e., you). Rather than producing value in exchange for money, you build something that creates more personal freedom for yourself. In most cases this means you earn money **and** time. It may also mean you earn connections and prestige.

Most people who run Freedom Businesses do so in order to achieve (or get closer to achieving) their ideal lifestyle, myself included. I wanted to be financially secure, location independent, well-connected, and in a position to be constantly trying and learning new things".

~ Colin Wright, excerpt from Start A Freedom Business

How much will it cost?

These days you can set up a business for less than $100. What's more, the money you put into looking more professional than you may feel, and presenting yourself as if you're bigger than you really are, will pay back dividends.

That may sound contrary to a lot of advice you'll receive, but hear me out. You have to treat your business as the success you'd like it to become, from the very beginning. Take yourself seriously and keep your eye on your grand vision. Always.

Clearly state your unique special proposition (USP) using great design, branding and communication. Initially this is hard to do as you are finding your way, but remember: 'Done is better than perfect'. So just start; you can continually tweak and improve along the way.

Where to spend your first dollar

There are plenty of services that let you build a business for next to nothing. Take advantage of them. If I was handed $100 today to start a business, here is how I would invest that money:

What .... **Cost**

A great domain name from NameCheap .... $10 one off

Domain hosting from Hostgator .... $6 monthly

WordPress Design (use Elance or oDesk) .... $50 one off

Logo design (through fiverr.com) .... $5 one off

Mentoring by a successful entrepreneur .... $10 lunch

PayPal Account to receive payments $0

e-Junkie account to sell digital products .... $5 monthly

3 Social Media profile designs (Fiverr.com) .... $15 one off

Total Spent **$96**

No need to break the bank is there? In fact, you should make your biggest investment in yourself: you will need to take the time to understand the psychology of online marketing, selling and influence.

Learn to become the best at what you do; improve your skills, pay for a mentor or for coaching. Set aside time to learn how to engage and market your brand through social media and how to become a better blogger to gain more credibility and drive leads and referrals.

The secret to doing what you love

If you're excited by what you've just read but are still wondering exactly what it is that you can do, be or build, you're not alone. Right now, when there are more opportunities than ever to build something out of nothing, people seem to be all hung up on what that 'something' should be. Some of the more regular excuses are:

- I have a gazillion ideas running through my head all the time but just can't figure out which one those to turn into a viable business;

- I'd love to have my own business but I'm just not sure I'm good enough at anything for people to actually pay me;

- I love doing this, and this, and this as well, but I can't decide how to pull that all together into something tangible that would make me a living;

- People tell me I'm really good at XXXX and that I should go into business and do it properly, but I'm just not sure. It scares the heck out of me.

Well guess what? These problems have been around for centuries. What it comes down to is our inability to get clear on what our gifts are and to whom we need to present them in order to profit.

When I started my blog I had no idea how it would turn out, only that I wanted to make it work. I hadn't figured out my "zone of genius", but I did have an insatiable appetite to learn and apply my marketing and business development knowledge to the online world.

I failed a lot. My ego got bruised and I frequently thought about giving up. Then, something changed. I started to get feedback from a small tribe of people who cared. They gave me the best gift of all. They told me I was doing a good job and to keep it up. I was actually making a difference by doing what I loved and by being me.

Do you know how amazing that feels? It's like all your birthdays have come at once. Somebody thinks you've done something valuable enough to take the time to tell you so!

And that, my friend, is the secret: there is no secret.

Be your very best self and success will, slowly but surely, come along on your journey with you.

And yet, we tell ourselves that being ourselves is not enough. We have to be AMAZING, incredible, adorable, off-the-Richter-scale smart and of course gorgeous, talented and special in order to be rich and fulfilled.

Bollocks.

That is not reality. That's an imaginary barrier you have built to sabotage yourself. It stops you from making the decision to play a bigger game than you are playing now. It stops you from putting yourself up on the pedestal that you deserve.

I'm not sure when we become so acutely aware of what **we can't do**. Perhaps every time we're told to "grow up"?

It seems that the more opportunities we're given, the more reasons we come up with to not jump on them. Nobody knows you better than you know yourself, but your awareness of your own limitations (real or imaginary) blind you from really knowing how brilliant you are.

How dare you not share your gifts with us! How dare you hide them away in your cupboard of fear and self-doubt? Let us see what you have and let us decide for ourselves, thank you very much!

Now that we have that sorted, I want to tell you how to shine.

The BIGGEST reason why people do not know what they really want to do is that they cannot figure out their *sweet spot.*

Your sweet spot is the intersection between what you love to do, what you are good at doing and what people will pay you for. Here's an exercise to help you find yours.

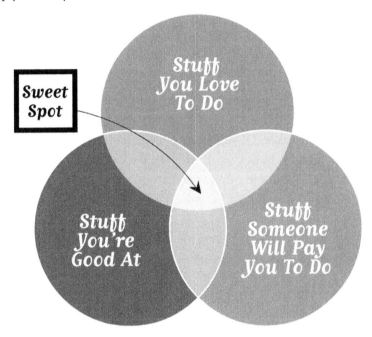

(I take my clients through this regularly, even those who already have businesses. It's a great exercise to come back to when you feel you're straying off course).

Four steps to finding your sweet spot

1. Know your fundamentals

Remember to focus on what you have, not on what you don't have. You don't need a lot of money or an MBA to start a small business. You *do* need a product or service, a group of people who want to pay for this service, and a method to receive the payment.

2. Know your strengths

Make a list of what you enjoy doing, or better yet, what you love doing. List as many things as possible. For example: dancing, sewing, painting, writing, speaking, solving IT problems, throwing parties, editing proposals, finding sponsors, pouring coffees, advising people on their next move, etc.

3. Listen to others

Make a second list, this time list what people tell you that you're good at. Stop dismissing their comments. When your friends or colleagues say 'You're really good at A) at organizing meetings, B) playing matchmaker, C) baking banana cakes, D) simplifying the complex, E) running raffles, F) choosing the right clothes, G) making people laugh, then listen to what they have to say. The people around you have recognized something in you that you may take for granted but which they find extremely useful and valuable.

4. Find the solution

Now take a look at your two lists and work out which are the ones that people need and pay for.

How to make money before you've even created a product

Any savvy entrepreneur will know that listening to what people are struggling with and then coming up with a solution to their problem, is a surefire way to succeed. In my own case, I had noticed lots of people asking me about the tools I used to run my business.

So I began to write the definitive book called The Ultimate Toolkit For Evolutionary Entrepreneurs, researching and profiling the best tools. I then approached the companies that I was writing about, to see if they wanted to pay a small sponsorship amount of US$150-250 be featured in the book.

I soon had $2,500 in sponsorship — before I'd even finished the book — as well as an early interest list of 150 people, which was proof enough that this project was worth doing.

I had taken those things that I enjoyed and was good at and had turned them into a profitable product that still sells. Naturally, working hard to hone my skills and to build a reputation was part of the process.

This may all seem "easier said than done". But get started by getting to know yourself and then you can turn your sweet spot into a fully blown candy store!

So what is YOUR sweet spot?

Two ways to make money online

Next, it's time to make sure your business model suits your personality type and the lifestyle you're designing for yourself. It's no gift to make loads of money but hate your work.

If you want to build an online business that allows you to work from anywhere, it's best to narrow the focus down to two proven methods that work well from a laptop and from no fixed location. These methods are:

1. **Selling yourself:** create a product, program or service that people want to buy and then sell it to them;

2. **Selling other people's stuff:** find a product or service that someone else has created, that people want to buy, and then sell that to them.

It's not rocket science!

#1. Selling yourself

I'm not talking about standing on a street corner here; I'm talking about selling access to the knowledge and skills you've acquired in your lifetime (even if you think you have none). This is one of the most exciting and natural ways to build a business you love.

You do that by becoming what has been known as a "Guru" or "Expert" and is now more commonly referred to as a "Mediapreneur".

> "There are tons of ways you can monetize yourself as a "mediapreneur" like products, programs, services, software, coaching, events, membership sites ... the list goes on and on and on.
>
> Here's the first not-so-secret secret: They all work. Here's the second not-so-secret secret: They all take effort and you should choose the ones that resonate the most with you and get YOU excited.
>
> Try one model and if you don't like it? The world doesn't end. Try again."
>
> ~ *David Siteman Garland, Rise To The Top*

Thanks to the Internet, the ways in which you can sell yourself have diversified to provide you with endless opportunities, as David points out.

These include marketing and selling yourself from your social media platforms, blogging, vlogging and podcasting. Or you can use live video-course platforms like creativeLIVE and Udemy where you can share your knowledge on just about any topic. The list continues, right through to charging to speak at conferences or running your own in-person work-shops and retreats.

> **Example: Sean Rogers** was fascinated by movement and martial arts and intrigued by the practice of Parkour. The more knowledge and time he invested in learning natural movement skills for himself, the more his friends and the people he met became interested too. Sean practiced Parkour for two years before being invited to teach classes with Fifth Ape, an outdoor Parkour and natural movement training business, which he did for two years. He got serious about blogging and created his website, **Prime8Movement.com** where he writes and creates videos focused on showing how movement and play can improve one's life. He has since created a book and a video course on Udemy covering the fundamentals of Parkour, in addition to teaching in-person workshops.

#2. Selling other people's stuff

While it's easier to get excited about selling your own products, you can be highly profitable selling other people's stuff as a distributor or an affiliate, if you do it well. This method of selling may appeal to you if you aren't up for putting in as much effort as selling yourself, because you don't have to create or build anything, you just market and promote the product. There are four ways to do this:

1. Selling digital information products like a program, course or book. You receive commissions as an affiliate, which is really like being an independent sales person earning commissions on what you sell.

> **My example:** From one webinar that I hosted with Clay Collins, I made $2,500 in sales commissions (it's a great product and he's an excellent marketer). The total time I used to promote the webinar to my list and through social media was perhaps 90 minutes over a few weeks, but it took me 3 years to build a reputation for sharing only high quality content and offerings.

2. Selling other people's physical products as a distributor or through a drop shipping service such as DOBA. You can pick and choose which products you'd like to brand as your own, or simply sell them directly from your e-Commerce site.

> **Example:** Britta Wein set up her own e-Commerce site **lunapads.de** to distribute women's products, made by the Canadian company Luna-Pads, throughout Europe. She buys the products at a wholesale price, pays to have them shipped from Canada to Germany and then sells them at a profitable retail value from her website and blog. She also sells into other online stores, and physical shops that want to stock the range of products. This is now her own independent business.

3. Selling other people's services by referring your customers/clients or friends to agencies, PR firms, web designers, personal trainers and the like. For doing this, you receive a referral fee or a commission. Once again, this can be accomplished through an affiliate program or an agreement you've made with the service provider in person.

> **My example:** I referred a client of mine to take up the **socialmedia-directbiz.com** services of Prerna Malik, giving her a glowing recommendation. My client took my advice and as a result Prerna sent me a generous percentage of the first month's contract amount.

4. Selling advertising. To make money from advertising online you need an established audience and a lot of traffic (i.e. thousands of visitors to your site, or more). Advertising is not something that you can just pop up on the side of your blog and make money from in a day. However, people do make a substantial amount from advertising affiliate products, allowing advertisers to buy space on their site to advertise products or services or even writing a sponsored blog post or review where the affiliation is disclosed to the reader.

Typically, the best way to create a viable business using advertising is through niche websites that, in their simplest form, are sites optimized for a specific niche. These sites need to attract a high volume of searches being conducted online by people like you and me and for a particular set of keywords, for example "green juice recipes".

The goal is to optimize your niche site to rank on the first page of Google and to receive a lot of visitors, who will then buy the products or click on your adverts. These sites take a lot of upfront work to build, a well-researched niche, as well as an understanding of online marketing, e-Commerce, SEO, Adwords and keywords.

Example: Pat Flynn is "the man" behind several profitable niche sites, and a role model for many starting out online wishing to make passive or residual income. As he puts it, after being challenged by a friend to build a niche site, within 73 days he was able to take **securityguard-traininghq.com** to #1 in Google for his target keyword and earn almost $700 per month. The site now earns approximately $3,000 per month and he's declined two buyout offers at $10,000.00 and $15,000.00. He has a number of other niche sites doing well too (plus a wildly popular blog, podcast and book).

So now that you have a better idea of what type of selling you're going to engage in and whether you're going to tweak your existing business model if necessary, how do you go about building your online business?

Six steps to building your online business

To run a a profitable online business, you need:

1. A One Page Business Plan

2. A website to sell you and your brand

3. A product or service to sell (yours or someone else's)

4. A content creation and traffic-driving strategy

5. A sales and marketing funnel

6. A set of systems to automate the grunt work.

These steps give you the foundation upon which to build your business. I describe them in detail in my book: BYOB: Build Your Online Business. What ultimately matters is that you build a freedom business, and for that you need to create a vision and a goal.

1. Your freedom business profit plan

1. **Set a vision:** Why do you do what you do? I suggest you watch Simon Sinek's excellent 'Start With Why' TEDx talk to help you think about this. Define the big "WHY" to create your vision, the "why" that's going to keep you going when you just want to give up.

2. **Set a goal:** Does freedom mean $1,000 a month to you or $1,000 a week? What do you need to feel you're free and happy? Set a goal for your annual revenue, e.g. $50,000, and profit, e.g $35,000.

3. **Set objectives:** No goal ever achieved itself, so break your goal down into key objectives. For example, to reach your revenue goal your 3 main objectives might be to:

    1) Build an engaged community of 500 email/ blog subscribers through regularly blogging about XYZ

    2) Create an online video training course

    3) Create a two-tier consulting service package and gain three new clients per month.

4. **Set a budget:** Based on your goals, you need to figure out your budget. Use my $100 breakdown near the beginning of this chapter and factor in any specific costs such as investing in software for landing pages, video creation and editing, or blogging optimization. Also factor in copywriting and design services. For the above example, let's make it $500 total.

5. **Set your revenue streams:** To reach your $50,000 revenue target stated above, it helps to break this figure down into monthly and weekly targets, for example, $4,134 each month and $961.54 each week. In order to break even on your initial start-up budget, you need to sell just over

$500 worth of something. You might get one sponsor for your blog for two months, sell 20 copies of your $25 video course or get 2 new coaching clients at $250 per session. Now run the numbers on what you need to sell each week to be profitable and you'll soon see if your revenue figure is achievable.

6. **Set a timeline:** You need to hold yourself accountable to deliver on your goals and objectives. When you break down your revenue streams, you must put a timeline next to them. If you don't they will not take on any sense of priority or urgency, and procrastination and perfectionism are the enemies of any business.

Luckily for you, you get my One Page Business Plan template to map out your freedom business. Yes, just one page. You can get that here: **suitcaseentrepreneur.com/book/resources**

Word to the wise

If you're just starting out and have nothing to sell, then you need to investigate and learn what customers will happily give you money for. Conduct a Google search for related products to those you are planning to offer and see what price point they have. If you think your product idea is unique, think again! I can almost guarantee it's been done before. This is a good thing. Remember to refer back to your sweet spot and then crunch your numbers to reach your revenue goals.

If you have an online business and have been selling products or services, you need to take a look at what your highest leverage and most lucrative profit streams are. Then you need to focus on which of these are doing well and how you can position yourself to command premium prices. Selling 100 units of a $390 product is far easier then trying to push 1000 units of a $39 product. Both result in close to $40,000 in sales.

2. A Website

Armed with your One Page Business Plan, you need a platform: somewhere to stand out and be found. This can be as simple as a landing page that states your offer and has a 'Buy Now' button or maybe a Facebook page.. Many profitable businesses have been built using these methods.

But I want you to go one better than that, and build a brand and platform you'll be proud of for years to come. This requires a simple website and ideally a blog. When you're starting out you probably won't want to spend too much money, but skimping on website design can be a costly decision in the long run.

It pays to spend more on great design and functionality, or to at least invest in regular upgrades as your business becomes more profitable. Put aside $300-$2,000 depending upon the level of complexity of design, how feature-rich you want your website to be and your budget.

Your website or blog ultimately needs to:

- attract, convert and sell prospects who visit

- be easy and inexpensive to manage and change – I highly recommend WordPress for any website

- clearly help your prospects achieve their most desired results.

A basic website should comprise:

- **A home page** that tells people in four seconds or less exactly where they've landed and why they should stick around. Your homepage should state your "WHY". It should make people want to sign up straight away for your newsletter.

- **An email opt-in form** where people can enter their email addresses to receive your weekly/monthly newsletter, and maybe your awesome free download (a video series, a book, an audio, or maybe a widget).

- **A Start Here page** that tells people in more detail why they're in the right place. It should include a compelling story that they can identify with and a summary of your best content; maybe that's just two blog articles, a short video talking about your "Why", or a short-list of resources (preferably your own) that dive deeper into your topic of "Mediapreneur-ness"

- **A Sales Page** so people can work with you or to buy from you. This can come later in your website's life, but you might as well have something on offer right out of the gate, even if it's a half an hour Skype consultation.

- **A Contact Page** that your soon-to-be-raving fans can use to connect with you, to give you more insight into what they need, or where sponsors and the media can email you. Some people would disagree with me on this, but you need to be approachable and you shouldn't make it hard for your visitors to hunt you down and connect with you.

3. Your product or service

The sales page on your website is going to need a product to sell. This can be one that you've designed yourself, a service offering you've formulated, or another product or service that you're selling on behalf of someone else. Whatever it may be, it needs to:

- be exactly what your customers most want to buy

- be exactly what you want to provide

- make your customers outrageously happy and help them get what they need.

To get this right will require testing, tweaking, continual improvement and a deep understanding of who you are targeting and what they want. If that were easy then everyone would be doing it.

Unfortunately (or luckily!), most people don't take the time to complete this basic and fundamental research, and therefore miss out on making lots more cash. I have written another book called Am I Your Customer? that dives deep into the heart of figuring out who your ideal customer is, narrowing your niche and lots more juicy information.

4. Content creation and traffic-driving strategy

Whether you have a website, blog, newsletter or Facebook page, you need to create a simple system for creating content which will:

- Generate trust and goodwill in your market

- Instantly establish you as the the go-to person in your field

- Create a natural and overwhelming desire for people to buy your products.

I recommend that you set up a calendar to schedule your content, covering your newsletter and the content for your blog, as well as the themes you will be talking about for each week and month. This calendar will keep you focused and on track. Handily, you can find a Content Marketing and Editorial Calendar template for just this purpose in the resources section.

The next step is to drive visitors to your site. People won't come just because it exists, you need to go out and find them.

So think about it; what's the first thing that you do when you want to find a product or service? Yep, you Google it! For this reason you need to use smart strategies to get your website to rank highly in the search engine results and to get found by potential customers.

You can do this by:

- Focusing on high quality lead generation through your social media platforms, videos, podcasts, free content and reports;

- Leveraging your time, energy and content for maximum results;

- Orchestrating a snowball effect that propels you and your business to have the maximum online visibility: being seen to be everywhere.

Once again, my BYOB Build Your Own Business guide (**suitcaseentrepreneur.com/byob**) is a great resource for more detail on these points, or you can come on over to my blog for a load of free resources, blog posts, videos and podcasts that show you how. (**suitcaseentrepreneur.com/entrepreneurs-blog**)

5. Sales and marketing funnel

A sales and marketing funnel ensures that visitors go into your website and money comes out. This funnel includes your blog content, collecting leads via opt-in forms or squeeze pages, creating your newsletter content, through to product launches, sales and follow-up.

In order to set this up you need to understand and implement timeless marketing principles that work in any industry and learn how to write great copy that turns words into money and the psychological triggers that make your customers feel happier, healthier and more empowered.

I highly recommend paying upfront for copywriting services and a sales page strategy session early on in your online business building process. You will learn so much in the process and sell more of your products as a result. For more in-depth guidance check out my BYOB Build Your Online Sales Funnel book (**suitcaseentrepreneur.com/byobsalesfunnel**).

6. Systems to automate the grunt work

When you put a system in place to manage all those moving parts, your business will run more smoothly and you'll make huge leaps in revenue (check out Chapter 9 for my suggestions on tools and services to make that easier).

Essentially what I'm talking about is mapping out the entire process a visitor to your blog or website goes through, from the first interaction with you and your brand, through to buying from you.

It takes time to build this automation system, but it's worth it. You will be able to step back from doing all these tasks yourself and hand them over to a team member as you build your business further (see Chapter 10 on outsourcing and building your virtual team).

None of this is easy. It requires dedication to learning, testing, failing, rebuilding and improving. This is the fun process of becoming a better marketer and it's just part of the journey to building a thriving online business.

Attempting to describe how to create a business from scratch – or how to leverage an existing business — is impossible in just one chapter. That's why I recommend you check out The $100 Startup from Chris Guillebeau, Start a Freedom Business from Colin Wright and Click Millionaires by Scott Fox, as well as the other books I mention in this chapter.

Here's to your success in creating freedom in business and adventure in life.

What can you do to build your own business now?

- Download the One Page Business Plan template and take 30-60 minutes to map out your Freedom business. (My BYOB Build Your Own Business book can help you further with this.)

- Look at your current online platforms. Consider how you can leverage what you currently have within a time frame of the next 30 days. Can you write an eBook, or package your knowledge into a key service, or create a landing page preselling for a program you're thinking of launching?

- Take time to work through the other templates provided to you for free at **suitcaseentrepreneur.com/book/resources**, particularly the online content marketing and editorial calendar. Even if you're not gearing yourself up to be a mediapreneur, it will still pay to understand your long-range plan to attract leads and generate new business.

- Pick up a copy of the books I recommended above and set aside a weekend to consume them, and this entire book, and take lots of notes!

Chapter 6

Becoming a citizen of the world and setting up an international business.

Whenever you find yourself on the side of the majority, it is time to pause and reflect.
~ MARK TWAIN

Disclaimer: I'm not a legal, tax or immigration expert so please consult with a professional before following any advice in this chapter.

Being a citizen of the world — a global nomad — presents some fasci nating challenges and opportunities.

At the time of writing, the world just isn't ready for location-independent types and that's why I was able to be a fiscal nomad for close to two years. Financial institutions are not set up to deal with the fact that you may have no fixed abode, physical address or permanent phone number.

Other service providers are not yet ready to deal with the transient nature of living and operating. This is great news for you, since you can take advantage of the system in many ways.

In this chapter you'll learn:

- How to harness the changing nature of doing international business online

- My path to Suitcase Entrepreneurship including the benefits and challenges

- What factors you need to consider when setting up an international business

- Where to set up your business and how to decide this

- Where my business landed – an example in action

- The best banking options for frequent travelers.

Welcome to the new world

International businesses used to belong solely to large multi-national corporations and the wealthy elite. Luckily for us mere mortals, the proliferation of online businesses has meant that anyone with a laptop, an idea and an Internet connection can start working in the world of international commerce (see Chapter 2 if you missed the four things you need to be free).

You can make payments online with a tap of your PayPal app, send and receive money through Internet banking and take photos of physical checks and deposit them virtually into your bank.

Heck, you can even bump' phones with someone to pay them! You can attach tiny appendages to your phone to take credit card payments. The world is your financial oyster!

Signing those all-important contracts or legal documents doesn't require you to be there in person either, thanks to cool contract tools like Our-Deal or freelance proposal software like Bidsketch, where you release your signature by drawing with a mouse on your screen or by typing in your name.

Whoever said that you must be in a meeting room, sitting across from a lawyer, banker or an accountant, was pulling your leg. In fact, it was probably someone in one of those three professions who told you, for fear of losing their day job. These in person' services are fast becoming obsolete, thanks to the technology and tools at our disposal.

International business planning

International business planning is a complicated and time-consuming endeavor. That means that advice in this area is often expensive and there are no "right" answers. You might visit five different attorneys and get five different suggestions, each one of which may be a good option.

The cost and ambiguity involved in planning an international business often results in many people simply tossing the whole idea out the window and winging it. That's usually my style, but as I've learned from hearing other peoples' horror stories, the consequences of poor planning or execution can be much more expensive.

Governments have far-reaching powers that normal creditors do not, so if you set up a tax-minimization scheme yourself and it proves not to be legally sound, you could end up owing a ton of money in back taxes, penalties and interest.

I owe big thanks to Kyle Durand, entrepreneur, lawyer and founder of Our-Deal, for helping me navigate my way through these problems. He takes a holistic and non-templated approach to building a business around your lifestyle and values – so you can see why I think the world of him and value his advice beyond words.

Kyle and I met online through the lovely Pam Slim (from Escape from Cubicle Nation) and then in person in 2012, when he took a chance on visiting me in Amsterdam. Luckily we got on like a house on fire, so visited him and his wife in Naples, Italy, a few months later.

We sat on the rooftop of the swanky hilltop mansion they were house-sitting and talked about the tricky landscape that online entrepreneurs and digital nomads face.

Later that year, Kyle joined Natalie MacNeil and me for our *Women Entrepreneurs Mastermind Retreat* we held on a cruise ship in the Caribbean. He ended up hosting a session on legal questions for small businesses that was a hit with the ladies.

Kyle is a lawyer, a tax specialist and also a digital nomad (from the US) who has worked with me to figure out my options. I am writing this chapter to give you some insight into how you might want to set up your business. But for specifics on your situation, I strongly recommend that you contact Kyle directly or read the book he is writing on this topic, which will be a perfect complement to this one.

My path to Suitcase Entrepreneurship

As someone with legal resident status in three countries, two passports and multiple bank accounts, I've been lost in this traditional system more than once.

So I'm offering myself up as a case study.

Like many online entrepreneurs, I started by simply launching a blog and selling products on my website. I was much more concerned with the design of my site and how PayPal would integrate with my shopping cart than I was about paperwork, taxes or bureaucratic formalities.

But, as my business began to grow, I became increasingly concerned about where the heck I should register my business and pay tax since it wasn't like I had a stationary storefront. Instead, my business had no geographic boundaries and my customers were from all over the world.

What makes my situation even more complicated is that I am a proud New Zealand citizen (although I haven't lived there since 2006), a UK Citizen (haven't lived there since 2008) and a permanent resident of Canada (haven't lived there since 2010). Although I have a legal status in three different countries, I am a non-resident for tax purposes in all three, because I've been absent from each nation for the required amount of time.

Things reached a crescendo for me in 2012. During that year alone, I was in New Zealand, Australia, eight different African countries, several European countries, the US and Canada, all while running my online business. The business income came in through my Canadian PayPal account and expenses were paid from that PayPal account and bank accounts in the UK, the US (yes even as a non-resident you can set up a bank account there) and Canada.

With so many different pieces to the puzzle (and a PayPal glitch), I realized that I needed to get a good handle on my business finances, administrative filings and tax requirements if I ever wanted to grow a sustainable business. The last thing I wanted was to build my business on shaky ground where some government agency could come along and tear it down because I hadn't followed the right procedures.

So, I went in search of answers, and here is what I found.

The challenges of being a digital nomad

Technology has evolved much faster than the law.

No one truly understands all the legal implications of being online. As the law rushes to keep up with the rapid shifts in technology, regulations have become even more ambiguous. Outdated laws and regulations use terms like "physical presence" and "nexus" to figure out where someone should register their business.

But permanent physical presence is almost impossible to determine for an online business run by a nomadic entrepreneur. We don't have a sign hung on a building somewhere, telling the world that we have something to offer.

The law needs to be interpreted.

Because there is little-to-no law specifically on this point, we, and the specialists who advise us, have to draw analogies between old situations upon which the laws were based and the new realities, and then assume that governments won't change their mind.

There are thousands of laws

Think about it; technological developments are so rapid that the laws of each and every nation can't possibly keep up with the advances. This means that approximately 196 nations (or so) have outdated laws, and each city or state or province is trying to apply old laws to a new business paradigm. Finally, add in all the different types of laws that apply to us as entrepreneurs – contract, privacy, intellectual property, tax, etc. – and you're left with a big ball of confusion and ambiguity.

Managing your business can be expensive.

If you are creative when establishing your business, it may cost you a bunch in government fees and legal and accounting expenses to set up and manage the business. For instance, setting up a corporation in Singapore will cost you around $5,000 for the first year and $5,000 for every year after that unless you know a local who will serve as your director. So, make sure to compare the costs of setting up and running your business in different jurisdictions to ensure the benefits are worth it.

"Setting up a company in Singapore is one of the better decisions I've made. I've helped entrepreneurs incorporate in many different jurisdictions around the world, but Singapore stands above the rest in terms of security, banking and financing.

It's a great place to migrate to and the Singapore government makes it easy to set up a business here. They provide incentives for hiring, training, and they have a special pass called an *entrepass*, which allows for a foreigner to access *ACRA* – the online portal where all companies are registered and maintained.

With a Singapore Private Limited Company you can also obtain a merchant account to charge credit cards. Essentially, Singapore is a great place to incorporate, and it doesn't matter whether you are bootstrapping backpack businessperson, an ambitious upstart seeking fundraising, an established business looking for a HQ overseas, or an investor seeking asset protection and high yields."

~ *Edmund John, FlagTheory.com*

The benefits of being a digital nomad

Liability protection

Entrepreneurs are faced with a variety of risks, and offshore planning may be a worthwhile mitigation tool, depending upon what you're doing. Good planning can help reduce the risk of exposing your hard-earned assets to liability. According to a recent study by Bolt Insurance Agency, more than half of the lawsuits brought against businesses in the United States affected companies making less than $1 million.

What's more, one out of every three business owners has been sued or threatened with a lawsuit in recent years and studies have shown that close to 94% of the world's lawsuits occur in the United States. It sucks to be part of that statistic; so international business planning can help mitigate the risk by moving some assets to places where they are harder to reach.

Privacy

In this increasingly connected world, where Google knows more about us than our own mothers do, you can understand why many of us want to protect our privacy. This goes beyond using a Virtual Private Network when we're online and protecting our passwords through encryptions.

I'm talking about the serious privacy of our business and financial matters. Many people are uncomfortable with having their personal information published as part of the public record. Several nations have made it a priority to lure international businesses with the promise of increased privacy. If this is important to you then the best bet is to do your due diligence and talk to an expert.

You can shop around

As a global entrepreneur, you get to choose (to a certain extent) which government's regulations best suit your situation. Why subject your business to one nation's expensive administrative fees, onerous reporting requirements and excessive intrusions into your privacy when you can take your business somewhere where it is cheaper and easier to operate and that offers more privacy?

You can save substantial amounts on taxes

The biggest financial benefit of international planning as a business owner is your opportunity to save on taxes. As long as there has been money, there have been people wondering how to keep hold of more of it, and saving on taxes is one of the biggest and best ways to retain more of your hard-earned money.

Most of us have heard of mysterious places called "tax havens" but figured that those were the sole realm of the ultra-rich or criminals. Not so fast! With the rise of the Internet economy, any of us who run an online business can legally take advantage of tax benefits offered by global financial centers.

Look at Apple: the poster-child for international tax planning. Apple is an American corporation but a global company, with 61 percent of its revenue from non-American operations. To legally minimize its tax, it set up subsidiaries in lower tax countries like Ireland and prevented at least $74 billion from being taxed by the US between 2009 and 2012. Now, I know we don't all run multi-billion dollar companies, but this is a sterling example of what can be done legally to save money with some good tax planning.

Where to set up your business

Sadly, there is no one "right" answer to the question: *"Where should I set up my business?"* There are too many factors to consider, too many variances in international laws, and everyone's situation is different.

You may be most interested in establishing your business in a foreign country because you want the benefit of a lower tax rate, whereas someone else may cite privacy as his or her biggest concern. So, what are some criteria to consider when establishing your business home?

Factors to consider

Your personal citizenship and residency

1. What is your nationality and what are that country's tax laws relating to citizens living abroad?

2. Where are you a resident taxpayer?

3. Where are your bank accounts and where do you hold your assets, both tangible and intangible?

Depending upon the answers you give to the questions above, you can legally minimize your tax situation by planning accordingly, doing your own due diligence, and consulting with experts.

Tax minimization

Of course, we all want to save money on taxes, but, be careful of falling into the trap of looking solely at corporate tax rates or using tax minimization as your only reason for choosing a place to register your business.

I know of many Americans who ran off and set up corporations in Singapore or Hong Kong because they had read on the Internet that the corporate tax rate was zero for income outside of the jurisdiction.

When I asked Kyle about this particular situation, he told me that several states in the United States also have zero corporate tax and that sole proprietorships, LLCs, partnerships, and S-corporations are not taxed by the federal government.

So, those Americans could have saved thousands in fees by registering their businesses in the U.S, especially given that those people would be subject to US personal tax anyway, since U.S. citizens are taxed on their worldwide income.

Taxes, and especially international taxes, are incredibly complicated. There are a ton of ways to save money on taxes, but they may not require you to register your business in a foreign country. So, remember to consider all of the contributing factors.

" You don't have to live in Wyoming to set up a Limited Liability Company (LLC) there — you just register your business there. You might still have to pay your state a "foreign corporation" fee to do business, but it's typically less than full incorporation. Wyoming's asset protection laws for single-member LLCs are very strong, and the state is solvent and unlikely to levy additional fees, which makes it a good option for a lot of small businesses, in the same way Delaware is a good option for financial companies and businesses that want to IPO.

~ Josh Kaufmann, from a Facebook post, showing you that this stuff is more involved than you think

Liability protection

Running a business is going to expose you to potential lawsuits. The amount of risk depends a great deal upon your industry. For instance, you are much more likely to be sued if you sell medical products than if you sell an eBook. Forming a limited liability business entity is only one way to protect your assets.

Privacy

How important is keeping your involvement in the business private? In many online ventures, the notoriety of the owner is the biggest draw to the business. If you are the face of the business, it doesn't make sense to then try to keep your name out of the public corporate documents.

Political and financial stability

One of the most important things to look for when deciding where to keep your money is the stability of the country and of the bank. A country that is regularly involved in political upheaval or that radically alters its financial and business policies is one to steer clear of. As for the bank, watch out for small offshore banks that may be inadequately capitalized. Subsidiaries and branches of major multinational banks, like HSBC, are a good choice when it comes to stability.

For years, the tiny Eastern Mediterranean island nation of Cyprus enticed wealthy individuals and businesses from all over the world to conduct banking in the island nation, with promises of high interest rates and low taxes. But many of those banks turned around and squandered their depositors' money on Greek junk bonds.

When the Greek economy hit the skids, the banks in Cyprus could no longer afford to pay their depositors the interest rates promised, and, in many cases, didn't have enough money to cover customer withdrawals. In the end, the government of Cyprus took a €10 billion bailout from the EU and introduced a scheme in which any customer with over €100,000 in an account stood to lose up to 40% of it to the government.

You want certainty, predictability, transparency and consistency in how the rules are applied when it comes to doing business internationally.

Administrative burden

Forget the burden of having too much stuff in your life; the last thing you want is a ton of administrative burden in your business. That's why it's smart to consider which countries have less of this when you're setting up your business.

A recent study by Bloomberg ranked the best countries to do business in, both economically and politically, with Hong Kong taking top honors followed by the U.S. and Japan.

Also consider the extra administrative burden of potentially dealing with more than one jurisdiction. For instance, if you are a US citizen, you will still need to file a US tax return. So, if you set up a business in a foreign jurisdiction, you may end up having to file more than one tax return, and I don't know many people who like calculating tax and filling out multiple tax returns.

Where my business landed

My head was bursting at the seams with all the information about where I should set up my business. I sat down and laid out the criteria and decided upon operating as a New Zealand sole trader (our version of the sole proprietor). Why?

Citizen and residency/ taxes: I am a New Zealand (citizen), UK (citizen) and Canadian (permanent resident) and none of these countries required me to pay income tax if I was out of the country for a certain amount of days each year.

If I registered a business entity in one of these three countries, I would probably need to pay taxes on my business income, though. So, it benefits me, from a tax perspective, not to create a separate business entity.

Liability protection: The products and services that I currently provide to my customers do not expose me to a high risk of being sued, and I limit my liability by using disclaimers, contracts and insurance. So, forming a limited liability company was not a huge concern for me.

Privacy: Since I am the face of my business, privacy was not a big concern of mine. But the sole trader option ended up keeping my name out of the public records anyway.

Political and financial stability: New Zealand has a stable government politically and financially.

Administrative burden: New Zealand is ranked as the easiest country to start and operate a business from, according to Inc. Magazine.

So, that's how the whole "Where should I register my business?" quandary shook out for me. It may seem silly that I ended up as a sole trader in my home country after all of the research, but I made the decision knowing that it was the best one for my circumstances.

Where to set up your bank accounts

If you've read this far and have found the tax and legal advice a scintillating read, then you're bound to enjoy my observations and perspectives on international banking.

People often ask me how I manage my money; banking, withdrawals and other fun financial stuff. As you now know, I live and breathe online payments and transactions. When I'm not conducting my transactions via PayPal, I'm transferring money between the various international bank accounts I have set up in countries where I have legal residence.

Where you set up a business will often affect where you set up your bank accounts. But you have a few options when it comes to overseas banking that can make your life easier.

Banking in your country of residence:

The benefits of having a local bank account is that you can set up a personal check account, savings account and business account from which to manage your finances. When it comes to using your local bank account overseas, you can usually withdraw money from ATMs using your debit card, ensuring that it's accepted internationally, of course.

In the worst-case scenario, your bank will charge you a fee each time you take out money from an ATM, up to US$5 max. I am usually prepared to take this hit for the convenience, so long as I can take out the maximum amount of cash possible to make it worthwhile. Don't fall into the trap of withdrawing just enough to see you through for a few days; you'll end up wasting money in bank charges.

You should also consider that you are likely to be charged a fee from the bank that owns the ATM too. This can be anywhere from peanuts up to US$5 again. This is almost always stated on the screen before the transaction, so you can choose to continue or cancel at that point. It pays to ask your bank which international banks they align with, if any, then seek out those ATM machines to avoid or minimize ATM fees.

Banking in an overseas destination:

You can always attempt to open a bank account in the country you're visiting, if you have a tax number or a resident permit for that nation. If you don't have this then you can choose a bank that's affiliated with one in your home country and approach them about opening an account.

When I was in the UK I opened an account with First Direct, an online bank that I love and that is owned by HSBC. When I moved to Canada, despite not being a resident there at the time, I was able to use my credit history from the UK to open an HSBC bank account immediately.

As much as I don't like their high fees, you should consider HSBC to be 'the world's bank'. It has branches in hundreds of countries and makes it fairly easy to set up new accounts around the world, once you've established credit history with HSBC in one country.

Banking via an offshore account

Despite what you may think from watching one too many James Bond movies, offshore accounts are a great option for the international entrepreneur. You can save a bundle on taxes, clear a higher return on your investment or simply keep your affairs private.

In many cases, offshore accounts are an option geared to the more wealthy, as some of these accounts have a minimum balance requirement, but this is not always the case and depends upon the bank.

You don't actually need to travel to open an offshore account, but you do need to provide original documents by post, such as a passport and utility bills. Once set up, you can email or phone instructions for wire transfers if there is no online banking option.

Here are a few of the more popular offshore banking options:

- **Swiss bank accounts** work just like your own bank account, except that most legal matters like divorce, taxes and bankruptcy are considered private.

- **Cayman Island** accounts are generally geared to corporations with large annual revenues and wealthy individuals seeking privacy. It's possible to open an account and keep your identity a secret. Cayman Island banks generally require the account holder to maintain a fairly sizable balance, and bank fees can be relatively high.

- **Singapore** is an attractive option as it has the lowest tax rate in Asia, and, if you play your cards right, any interest you earn in Singapore can be tax-free.

- **Luxembourg** is a very stable and tax-free country, and has great returns on investment for deposit holders, although less so for European Citizens.

Wrapping it all up

Unlike the traditional shop owner, you, the nomadic entrepreneur, have a wide variety of options as to how you will set up and manage your business and financial matters.

Setting up an international business is generally not a simple matter, but the benefits can be great if you plan ahead and take into account what is most important for your particular situation.

Recommended reading and resources

My advice would be to consider what you've learned in this chapter, then consult these relevant links to do your own research, and then consult with an expert. You can find links to the below sites at **suitcaseentrepreneur. com/book/resources** Chapter 6.

• Business requirements in the EU

• Economy rankings based on ease of doing business

• Global tax links

• Kyle Durand's site

Your next steps to financial freedom

• Consider your upcoming plans for short or long term travel and whether you really need to setup a separate entity for your business

• Research the destination(s) you have in mind to make sure you will not run into any trouble with laws and regulations related to operating an online business, taxes and immigration.

• Ask your bank about their international setup and fees and consider switching to an international bank like HSBC.

• Consult with a trusted advisor or lawyer if you think that setting up an offshore company might be the best thing for your situation.

Chapter 7

The best systems and online tools to run your business from anywhere.

High achievers spot rich opportunities swiftly, make big decisions quickly and move into action immediately. Follow these principles and you can make your dreams come true.

~ ROBERT H. SCHULLER

Imagine the day when printers, desks, staplers, whiteboards, and even office walls don't exist. Wouldn't that be great?

Well we're almost there. Today, a laptop, or smartphone and an Internet connection are all we need. Everything else can be done online. In this chapter I'll show you how.

In this chapter you'll learn:

- The only tools you actually need to run your business from anywhere

- Setting up your systems to be location independent

- What you need to set up your virtual office

- Your business Department Breakdown.

The only tools you actually need to run your business from anywhere

If you twisted my arm and asked for the bare minimum of tools that you need to run your freedom-based business, I would happily recommend:

1. Google – everything: Gmail, Drive (formerly Docs), Apps, Google Plus, Google hangouts and Google phone number

2. PayPal – send and receive payments, set up a shopping cart online, transfer money between banks, use their payment card like a credit card, and turn your smartphone into a payment processor

3. Dropbox – cloud storage solution to house all your important files, photos, videos etc. and synchronizes across all your devices

4. WordPress – the gold standard platform upon which to create a website, blog and shop-front in one hit

5. Namecheap – where you can buy a domain name, host your website and back it up

Yes just five tools and you can do virtually everything that a major corporate can do and for less than $100. For a breakdown of how you can set up a business for under $100 check out Chapter 5.

Setting up your systems to be location independent

Ultimately, when it comes to setting up your virtual office and running your business from anywhere, you need to prioritize the key functions that your business model requires on a daily basis. Aim to automate those first, or have them run as seamlessly as possible. Then you can work on the rest.

"I was asked this morning what the best marketing system is for small businesses. My answer? It's the ONE THAT YOU USE.

The same goes for technology. What's the best CRM for small business? It's the one that you actually use. What's the best project management software? It's the one that you use. But we make it tougher than that. We have an aversion to learning to use the tools, courses, information and resources that are already available to us.

Instead we look for the next thing to cure our ills, make us thin, make us rich or make us more attractive to the opposite sex. Part of it is bright-shiny object syndrome, for sure (ooh look! a rabbit!) but it goes deeper, too.

When we admit that we have all we need to do our jobs and grow our businesses, we run out of excuses.

To run an online business you need a phone, a computer and a bank account. The rest is up to you and your personal preferences.

So take advice, act on it, and stick with it.

~ Matthew Kimberley, author of How to Get a Grip

I agree with Matthew entirely. With so many new and exciting tools being thrown in our face on a daily basis, it gets very easy to be distracted by the next bright shiny object (hey, we are entrepreneurs after all!).

It pains me to see people always looking for the next best thing, rather than consistently using tools that work well together so you can stop chasing rainbows. So that's exactly what I've put together for you in this chapter.

You are more than welcome to try out new tools that look as though they might serve a purpose in your business, so long as you actually make use of the free trial, evaluate whether it really was a critical or life-changing tool for you and your current systems set up, and then either adopt it or drop it. That's it.

Less is more when it comes to systems, tools and platforms. Choosing tools that integrate with each other is the number one tip that I can give you to save time and money. There's nothing worse than switching over to a feature-rich CRM system and then finding out that it doesn't work with the other key tools you use every day.

Systems are not just tools and software either, they're also the processes and standard operating procedures you put in place, which I discuss in more detail in Chapter 9. Here's my example:

> When I decided to ride 6,500km across Africa in March 2012, it was a real test of the systems I had put in place for my online business. I was nervous that being offline for almost two months was going to muck everything up, but ultimately I set up my business model to give myself more freedom. I didn't open my laptop for the first 3 weeks and only checked email briefly after one week to tell my friends and family that I was alive.
>
> I had to trust in my systems and in my virtual assistant, who I had hired and had handed everything over to, just two weeks before I had left. Here's how:
>
> • My virtual assistant was given a series of video tutorials on my blog publishing routines, newsletter campaigns and email responses.
>
> • I prepared a bunch of guest posts, content for my own site and podcast interviews in advance, then used WordPress to schedule them.
>
> • I told my coaching clients that for two months they'd only get email coaching (which had been a proviso when they had originally signed up).

- Community building and social media management tasks that were straightforward like scheduling tweets, sharing blog posts and posting images or podcasts were handed over to my VA.

- Wherever possible on the trip I'd check in either from internet cafes or by using data from other riders' iPhones. I'd update my followers on my progress by posting photos, saying "hello" from the road, sharing some insights and responding to comments, notifications and messages.

The results? Aside from less growth than normal in my community during that period, everything else ran like clockwork. Despite what you may think, people don't really miss you as much as you imagine, and life goes on without you!

So let's look at how to set up your business to work from anywhere.

Virtual office setup

When you set up a physical office, you consider such questions as: Do we need to get a landline? How many phones should we install? How much does new office furniture cost? Do we need filing cabinets? You can see your costs adding up before your eyes and it's scary, especially if you're not turning a profit yet.

As a virtual business owner with no office, you save big time on your set up costs. All your activities, meetings and projects can be virtual and you can set up systems to manage your business and team that can be accessed anywhere and anytime, transcending time zones and international borders.

So what tools do you really need? Well, you can look at a physical office and translate it into a virtual office pretty easily.

Reception:

- **oDesk** and **Elance** are your go-to online workforce communities for hiring competent freelancers or permanent virtual staff to get the job done and act as your reception staff.

Phone number

- **Grasshopper** as your virtual entrepreneur phone system people can reach you on, complete with voicemail.

- **Skype Personal Number** is a simple solution for your own number and voicemail capability, as is **Google Voice** for US only

Mailing address

- **Gmail** can handle all your email needs and you can set up multiple email accounts for you, your virtual assistant and your various departments like marketing@ or sales@

- To avoid paper mail select paper-free versions for everything including statements and bills. Most online banks and utility companies have this option now and this avoids having to open mail altogether.

- Use the Post Restante service at your local post office when you're traveling. All you need to do is produce a passport or form of ID to collect your mail, which will be addressed to FAMILY NAME (in capitals, First Name, Post Restante, City, Country.

- If you choose to rent a desk or work from a co-working space, they often have a service whereby you can have a mailbox, phone number and fax number for the time you're there.

Desktop:

- **Google Everything** — Gmail, Google Drive, Google Calendar, Google Apps – emails, online shared documents, drafts, forms, and scheduling

- MS Office or **OpenOffice** – for all your writing and presentation and spreadsheet needs

- **NeatDesk** and Neat's cloud and mobile services are actually designed for a real office or co-working desk to gain back both valuable office space and time lost searching for information in inefficient, outdated filing cabinets.

Filing cabinets

- **Dropbox** cloud storage is your filing system for photos, videos, files and important data, stored in the cloud and synchronized across all your devices. Accessible at anytime, from any computer, your mobile or their website.

- **AmazonS3** is an alternative to Dropbox, loved by many, especially for paying as you go and for what you use.

Meeting rooms

- **Skype**, especially their Premium account, is great for video conference calls and group screen sharing

- **Google Hangouts** also work for customer and client video meetings or product demonstrations

- **MeetingBurner** is a great webinar and online meeting platform that you can use to present to many or one, record video and audio and capture leads

All in one

- **Bitrix24** which is like Yammer (social enterprise) plus BaseCamp (project management) plus Zoho (CRM) plus DropBox, plus Skype and a few minor things (calendars, planners, work reports, Gantt charts, etc.) all rolled into one. This social intranet service is 100% free to small companies.

Business department breakdown

Online tools, software and services are my guilty geek pleasure. As a result I like to try new tools that will optimize my current system and make me more productive, profitable and free. After all life is short.

For this reason, I'm giving you the top level, must-have, must-try tools, but not fifteen versions of tools that all do the same thing. These are my opinions based on what works. Less is more. Ultimately it's up to you to choose the tools that suit your needs and make you feel like a rock star who's in control of all the moving parts of their business and their life.

Financial department

- **Shoeboxed** lets you send receipts, business cards and documents to them via postage-paid envelopes or camera-equipped smartphone for a really low monthly fee. They scan and data-enter every document, then organize everything in a secure, searchable online account.

- **Freshbooks** is your financial accounting and invoicing system, time and expense tracker and perfect for managing your clients and contractors.

- **Xero** online accounting software is when you're ready to step into your big business shoes and enjoy a full-featured web based system for invoicing, accounts payable, bank reconciliation & bookkeeping.

Website design and e-commerce department

- **Hostgator** allows you to choose from a range of website hosting plans and delivers a variety of services including setting up your own website.

- **Namecheap** offers some of the most affordable domain names in the industry, in addition to fully featured web hosting packages.

- **WordPress** is web software you can use to create a beautiful website or blog and manage your online content

- **LeadPages** is the easiest way to create beautiful landing pages, launch pages, sales pages and squeeze pages for your website that actually convert.

- **Optimize Press**. also lets you build customized landing pages, but more importantly it also allows you to create membership sites to host your programs and courses.

Marketing and social media department

- **Hootsuite** is your all-in-one social media dashboard that allows you to post and schedule updates to multiple social media platforms at once, as well as track keywords, hashtags, lists and your analytics.

- **Mailchimp** makes sending out a newsletter amazingly easy. Design and send beautiful emails, manage your subscribers and track your campaign's performance. Equal alternative is **Aweber**.

- **InfusionSoft** is a robust solution to really turn your business into a serious sales and marketing machine, as well as handling email management and lead generation

- **WiseStamp** is an email signature tool that transforms your boring email into clever branding for your business. You can link your social media profiles, blog feed, videos and more into your signature or you can even use it to sell products.

- Social Media platforms including Facebook, YouTube, Twitter, Google-Plus, LinkedIn and Pinterest

- Google Adwords, Facebook Advertising, Twitter Advertising are great for getting the word out

- **AdRoll** is an effective retargeting platform to allow your ads to be seen in all the right places based on your ideal customer. **Perfect Audience** is another retargeting platform, but for Facebook.

Sales Department

- **PayPal** business or premium account lets you link your bank account and credit card and is the easiest way to set up payments for goods and services.

- **e-Junkie** lets you sell your digital products and programs for a monthly $5 fee, simply by creating a new product, uploading a digital file or pointing to a page on your site, and naming your price.

- **Gumroad** lets you sell directly with a link; you don't even need a website or PayPal account. Great for creative people to sell their goods.

- **Zoho CRM** gives you a 360-degree view of your complete sales cycle and pipeline so that you can keep track of your existing and potential clients, leads and sales opportunities too.

Customer service department

- **Zendesk** is a cloud-based customer service software that takes customer communication from anywhere—your website, email, phone, Twitter, Facebook, and chat—and turns it into a ticket for you and your support team to deal with.

- **Wufoo** lets you create customized and branded professional feedback forms and surveys. Google Forms does the job too but with less pizazz.

- **Google Hangouts** are a great way to hold live group calls with customers and clients for tutorials, Q&A or focus groups.

- Social Media in general through platform analytics and search functions as well as **Google Analytics**

- Tracking and social mention monitoring tools like Google Alerts mentioned in Chapter 9.

Human resources and legal department

- **OurDeal** is great for creating, sending and electronic signing of agreements and contracts within seconds

- **Bidsketch** allows you to customize proposals for clients (especially freelancers), cutting down the time you spend preparing them and using digital delivery and signoff.

- **Hello Fax** is a digital faxing solution that stops the need for you to have an office and from having to download attachments, print them, sign them and fax/scan them back.

- **LastPass** allows you to store all your passwords safely and securely in one location, as well important data like bank accounts, and you only ever need to remember one password. You can also securely share logins (without revealing passwords) with team members.

Team management and productivity department

- **Asana** is a free project and team management tool that allows you to create projects and assign and track tasks, leave notes, links, upload documents and it is free.

- **Rapportive** is a handy app that works right inside Gmail, giving you a real time report of who the person is who's emailing, including their name, picture, location, company and social media accounts. Great for networking, marketing and customer service needs.

- **SaneBox** takes unimportant emails out of your inbox, puts them in a separate folder and aggregates them into a daily summary so that you can focus on what's important. One-click-unsubscribe, follow-up reminders, sending emails later, and deferring non-urgent emails are great features too.

- **Evernote** allows you to organize your thoughts, web clippings and notes into a handy cloud storage system that synchronizes across devices

- **ScheduleOnce** is a meeting and appointment scheduling software that increases customer satisfaction, creates a smooth process for clients, and saves you messing with international time-zone confusion

- **RescueTime** is a productivity tracking tool which you install on your device. It monitors your every move and then shows detailed reports about what you spent your time on and where you can optimize your current routines to save an average of 3.5 hours a week.

Combining these tools together

Seeing all these great tools broken down may be useful, but how do they help your daily activities? Well, throughout this book I mention several of these tools for specific purposes, especially in Chapter 4 on the Future of Work, in Chapter 8 on Social Media and in Chapter 9 on Outsourcing.

If you take the time to read, or re-read, those chapters, you can see how many of these tools either work together seamlessly, or integrate and communicate with each other, to help you run a more streamlined online business.

You'll find that it will become even more common for software to integrate with other software, and you can use this functionality to your advantage to access a bigger piece of the customer market. A great example is Freshbooks, which has a number of application add-ons, so that you can easily transfer and work with your existing setup. For example you can use Freshbooks with Indinero, Bidsketch, Wufoo, Mailchimp, PayPal, Google, Zendesk and Highrise.

Your daily work routine

At the beginning of this chapter I mentioned five tools I could run my business with. If I break down the key tools I use on a daily basis, for my business model setup, it goes like this:

1. **Google docs** for editing and writing blog posts, guest posts, new product content, strategy and standard operating procedures

2. **Gmail** for responding to and sending emails, and within that Sanebox that works away at reducing my email overwhelm, and Rapportive that automatically pops up in my email sidebar

3. **Asana** for taking key tasks for the week and scheduling them under my ongoing projects and assigning team members

4. **Hootsuite** for checking on all social media engagement, mentions and monitoring as well as scheduling out a few key messages that are not already going out via TweetAdder (already set up by my GVA in advance)

5. **PayPal** mobile app for instant notifications about money going in and out, (luckily more of the former)

6. **Dropbox** to access additional files not stored in my laptop

7. **Infusionsoft** to check in on snew leads, email campaign stats, product sales and affiliates

8. **Skype** to connect with friends and hold meetings, interviews or coaching sessions

9. **WordPress** to draft and schedule blog posts and podcasts and to respond to comments.

In Chapter 10 I go into greater detail of how to set up a daily MIA (Most Important Action list) and create a routine that will allow you to create boundaries to get real work done.

Your day my look completely different depending upon what your focus is. Whatever you do, make sure that you focus on creating more freedom in business so that you can enjoy more adventure in life.

How to become more productive right now:

• Create a checklist of tools you're currently using most often, on any given day and evaluate whether they're saving you time and money or frustrating you.

• Look at the list of tools recommended in this chapter and see which ones would be good additions to your current ones and which would fit in best with your systems and budget.

• Take time to continually optimize your time spent running your business, and learn to use the tools at your disposal efficiently (if you try new tools really put them to the test and then quit using them if they don't serve a purpose).

• Checkout my definitive list of tools page on my website, which is constantly being updated at **suitcaseentrepreneur.com/tools.**

Chapter 8

How to use social media as your marketing, sales and customer service team.

It takes 20 years to build a reputation and five minutes to ruin it. If you think about that, you'll do things differently.

~ WARREN BUFFET

Having built my entire business using social media I feel very fortunate for its existence. So when I meet people that think it's a waste of time or don't get it, I tell them to wake up! These powerful tools allow you to build an online platform like never before.

If there's one thing you need to take away from this chapter it's this: your customers are hanging out on Facebook, talking on Google Plus and watching YouTube videos. If you're not right there with them, then you're missing out on abundant opportunities to engage, educate and profit. Got that?

If you're already blogging and tweeting but not seeing results, you might not have the right strategy in place.

There's a misconception about how to give and take value from these platforms. A lot of people just don't get it. Done correctly, social media can be your marketing, sales and customer service platform rolled into one.

In this chapter you'll learn:

- What is the point of social media?

- How to gain new business and make money on social media

- How to set up your own social media strategy

- How to track and monitor your results to optimize your strategy.

What is the point of social media?

Social media is the platform for your personal brand. It carries your voice to millions of people who need to hear your message. It's a place to engage and connect with some of the smartest and most progressive minds in the world. It's home to your friends, family and people you've not even met yet.

It's your life online.

So how do you use social media to gain trust and credibility, to build a community, generate leads, increase traffic and actually make sales?

Be yourself. Be helpful. Be outstanding.

In Chapter 5 we went through the three main options for making money online — selling your own products, those of others or selling yourself as a mediapreneur.

Regardless of whether you want to be the face of your business or not, you are still your own personal brand and every interaction you make online needs to reflect your brand values.

In his book microDOMINATION: How to leverage social media and content marketing to build a mini-business empire around your personal brand, Trevor Young writes about a new breed of entrepreneurs he dubs micro mavens', who leverage the power of social media and content marketing to develop their own platform and build their personal brand on a global scale.

Trevor showcases micro mavens who have done this in their own unique way, people like Chris Guillebeau who has built a 'small army of non-conformists', Gary Vaynerchuk and his wine-loving aficionados and even me, with my freedom seeking rebels and fellow Suitcase Entrepreneurs.

> "Micro mavens grow their community, or tribe, of fans, followers and advocates of their ideas and what they stand for, by being real, authentic and allowing people to share in their journey or story they're creating.
>
> "Micro mavens tailor their business to fit their lifestyle. As a result, they create and build businesses with multiple streams of income – speaking, coaching, publishing e-books or online courses, training programs, or running virtual or physical events.
>
> "Thus, the cornerstones of the micro maven are (a) develop your platform, (b) build your personal brand, (c) grow your multi-income business, and (d) live your dream lifestyle."
>
> ~ *Trevor Young, Micro Domination*

Everything you post will be online forever, so make sure every interaction counts. If you want to build a thriving online business, you need to stand up and be noticed for the right reasons. This does not mean spamming people with messages, adding them to your email list without their permission or constantly talking about yourself.

Nope, this means building trust through engaging with your friends, networks and potential customers; it means adding a ton of value, being helpful and providing insight, education and inspiration on a daily basis. It sounds simple, yet so many people get this wrong.

"The people who have chosen to follow you on social media will have more of an impact on your success and your income than almost anyone else. Call them your tribe, or your 'followers'; in practical terms they are the people who sign up to your email list or who hit like on your Facebook page.

"Here is why they matter: they are the people who will buy what you have to offer and/or spread the word about what you're offering so that others buy it. Not only that; they help you create the right products. Listen closely and they will give you information about what they actually want you to be offering them in the first place. When these valuable people do you the honor of allowing you to pop up in their Google Plus stream, or to make an appearance in their already crowded inbox, how should you treat them?

" **Treat them like you DO give a damn.**

"This is the part most people forget when dabbling in social media 'for profit'. Social media is not the online equivalent of a giant billboard by the side of the highway and it is not an updated version of old-style website banner ads.

"1. Treat your followers like humans. 2. Give a damn. If the whole idea of social media overwhelms you, use these two principles as your starting point and you'll supercharge the success you have with every tactic you learn in this book."

~ *Marianne Cantwell, Free Range Humans*

Benefits of social media for business

If you need further proof that social media is powerful, then here's some of that proof:

Social Media Examiner is a blog for learning social media. Their 2013 Social Media Marketing Industry Report shows that businesses who use social media achieved the following, ranked by highest percentage:

1. Increased exposure

2. Increased subscribers, traffic and your opt-in list

3. Generated new business partnerships

4. Increased search engine rankings

5. Generated qualified leads

6. Reduced overall marketing expenses

7. Closed more business.

Let me add that using social media will also help you to:

- Demonstrate thought leadership

- Build your reputation and credibility

- Provide real-time customer support

- Drive existing and prospective customers to your content

- Sell your products and services across multiple platforms

- Generate and increase word-of-mouth buzz for your business

- Get you more of your ideal customers.

How does this happen?

Well aside from witnessing it daily myself, much research by agencies shows that:

- 33% of people visit social media sites to engage in product research before making a purchasing decision

- 47% of consumers let social media sites influence their decision to purchase specific companies' services & brands

- 26% of potential customers change their minds about purchasing a product after reading about it on a social media site.

So now do you want to get in on a piece of that action?

How to use social media platforms to actually get more business and sales

The great news is, there are so many people who need your help and, guess what, they're all hanging out online talking about their problems. You just need to listen, learn and then act. I've hired several people as a result of connecting on social media and I've also received a lot of new business.

Below, I give you tangible methods to apply in order to gain new business and some fantastic examples from others who've seen success in doing these things.

I've focused on some of the top social media platforms, which many consider to be blogs (WordPress, Blogger or Tumblr), Facebook, Twitter, LinkedIn, GooglePlus and YouTube. Of course there many other contenders like Pinterest, Instagram and Quora and approximately 550 other social media sites, a number that continues to grow.

But you don't have to be on every single platform. You need to be:

- where your customers are hanging out

- on the platforms that you feel most comfortable with using

- on the sites that make sense to you, your brand and your business.

That's it. Trying to do anything more will overwhelm you.

Want to find out where your customers hang out?

- Ask them

- Search for them on the main networks

- Google them and see what search results come back.

Direct Engagement on Facebook

Cheryl Wood is a member of the Facebook Book Marketing Group which I set up to allow people to follow the journey of this very book you're reading. One day I was in a slight panic about getting everything done and I asked "Who do you recommend, who does great book cover designs?" Cheryl, who is a designer, piped up first, messaged me through Facebook, jumped on a Skype call with me and got the contract to design my Kickstarter guide cover within 24 hours.

How to do this for yourself:

Take 20 minutes each day to read your Facebook news feed and interact within the groups you're part of. Look at what questions people are consistently asking. If you see a question like "Does anyone know a good virtual assistant?" and that is what your business is, then act accordingly and contact them with how you can help, both in a comment and personal Facebook message. Be proactive.

Gaining attention on Twitter

"I use Twitter lists to follow reporters, writers, and editors. I regularly interact with these people so that I'm on their radar for when they are working on a story relevant to my expertise. If reporters and editors know who you are and what you're all about, there's a much better chance you'll get asked to give quotes for pieces they are working on.

"An editor I had been following and engaging with from Forbes first reached out to me via a Twitter Direct Message to get me involved with Forbes Woman, which is an outlet that continues to be one of the top ten traffic drivers to **SheTakesOnTheWorld.com** and another reporter from People Magazine reached out to me through an @Reply on Twitter. I followed up and landed myself in the print edition of People StyleWatch. These kinds of press opportunities would cost a fortune if I was paying a publicist to get them for me."

~Natalie MacNeil, Founder of She Takes On The World

How to do this for yourself:

1. Curate your Twitter feed in a way that is attractive to the media. MacNeil suggests you do this by coming up with your own quotes that people will want to share, tweeting juicy sound-bites, and focusing on posting things that are highly relevant to your niche and area of expertise.

2. Do a simple search on **search.twitter.com** and put in a few key words related to what you do. Behold! Here is a bunch of people crying out for a new web design, a great copywriter or a new personal trainer. Engage with them on Twitter and tell them how you can help, but don't hit them with a hard sell right then and there. Be sure to follow up through a Direct Message and via email.

3. Update your Twitter profile to reflect your brand and use your profile page to market what you do so that people know in an instant how you can help them.

4. Link the URL on your Twitter profile directly to a specific landing page on your website, thanking people for coming to your site from Twitter and listing useful links about who you are, what you do and how you can help.

Building your expertise on LinkedIn

"As a marketing and business development consultant for professional services, LinkedIn is the perfect platform for me, as that's where my clients — primarily law firms and accounting firms - are. In fact it's now my second largest source of new business after existing clients. Even though I'm based in New Zealand my clients are local and international

Over the last six months I've gained four new clients, had six paid speaking opportunities and received 70% of my total revenue from LinkedIn. In fact I've built my profile as a LinkedIn specialist in my industry and regularly blog about it and produce videos on new features people can take advantage of. I even wrote a book on LinkedIn for lawyers. That's one way people find me and want to work with me. That's a huge shift in the way we now do business.

I also produced a free report that was requested by over 200 LinkedIn members. It drove a tremendous amount of traffic and new subscribers to my blog as well as accounted for around $50,000 of new business too. LinkedIn has totally changed my life."

~Kirsten Hodgson, Kaleidoscope Marketing

How to do this for yourself:

1. Spend 30-60 minutes a day engaging with and answering questions on relevant LinkedIn groups which you've joined, specific to your industry or niche

2. Focus on helping others, creating and curating content that's useful to your clients and sharing theirs in return

3. Post interesting links in your status updates and to industry groups, that either lead back to a blog post you have written that's on topic, or to a landing page for a free report (like in Kirsten's example above), driving new leads from interested prospects

4. Make sure your LinkedIn Profile and your LinkedIn Company page are always up to date with your latest bio, expertise, experience and product and service offerings

5. Encourage your current clients to leave you a testimonial on LinkedIn (and offer to do the same for them or others in your network) as proof of your greatness. Save effort by copying these over to your website too.

Example 3: Responding via email

Filipe Dinis had been reading my Highflyer email newsletter for months and one day hit reply to pay me a lovely compliment and congratulate me on my book progress. He mentioned he was from Portugal and had built his DesignHandyMan business from working with international clients. He went on to mention that if I ever needed graphic design work, a book laid out or website design, he'd be honored to work with me. Filipe got my attention. I checked out his site, liked what I saw and a few days later I hired him to design the interior of my Kickstarter guide. Right time. Right approach.

How to do this for yourself:

1. Understand who your ideal client is and when you come across them online, join their community by subscribing to their newsletter if they offer one. Learn more about how they work and what they need.

2. Craft your message appropriately and then, when the time is right, reply to an email of theirs (or reach out to them via the contact form on their website). Use your inside knowledge to offer your help on their project.

3. If you don't hear back from them, follow up in a week. Don't be put off. They may be very busy or receive way too many emails or have missed your message.

Example 4: Networking outreach

Karl had been reading my blog and following me online. Here's what happened in his own words, taken from a blog post he later wrote:

"I commented on Natalie's blog and then emailed her because I was a fan and wanted to engage with her. I offered to help improve the conversion rate on her flagship product BYOB, Build Your Online Business. She loved the idea and we set-up a time to dissect her sales page weaknesses and, at her suggestion, went on to create some video content to help her readers. Natalie won because I helped her improve her sales page conversion rate and I won because I was introduced to her audience and gained new clients from a webinar we ran together.

"People who can help your career or business are usually hinting at projects and concepts that you can help them with, so listen to what they need and be ready to offer your help when appropriate. They key is to be very enthusiastic with your offer. You are selling yourself. So don't be afraid to toot your own horn. I would suggest within your email you link to your testimonial page (if you don't have one, create one)."

Karl Staib, Domino Connection

How to do this yourself:

1. Follow people online whom you admire and with whom you want to align both yourself and your business. Join their community by subscribing to their blog feed, commenting on their posts and being an active participant to attract their attention.

2. Hit them up with your value proposition, but make sure you show that you actually care about the work they do by first citing recent posts, videos or interviews.

3. Make it easy for them to say yes to you by offering up something for free or, by offering a win-win situation that you take control of and that benefits their community or clients.

Example 5: Establishing your expertise

I ran a Kickstarter Campaign to raise awareness and funds for this self-published book. That wasn't all. I went on to write three helpful blog posts and to produce two podcasts which focused on how to use crowd funding to turn your dream idea into reality. As a result I got a lot of great feedback and many people asked me questions about what it takes to run a great campaign. So I wrote a guide on it and before it was even finished, had pre-sold a bunch of copies for people who couldn't wait to read it. I also had three clients reach out to me a few weeks after my campaign to work with them one-on-one. This was a whole new business angle I hadn't considered.

How to do this yourself:

Let's use the example that you're into fitness and healthy eating. So you choose to become the smoothie expert by learning as much as you can (be a leading learner as I discussed in Chapter 4).

1. Focus your social media efforts on being the go-to person in your niche, and make that as narrow as possible, something like green smoothies.

2. Post weekly videos (either with yourself in them or filming the ingredients and actual smoothie creation) on your blog and on YouTube.

3. Create a free report with some sample recipes and tips for staying healthy that people can access through your website and at the end of blog posts.

4. Create a paid recipe book that contains embeds of your most popular videos and links to the recipes. Sell this from your blog, website and social media channels.

5. Create consulting services or group coaching programs to teach enthusiasts how to make their own great green smoothies.

Setting up your social media strategy

The number one reason you'll fail to see any results from using social media as your marketing, sales and customer service department is because you don't have a strategy or goals or objectives in place. Get these things right and all your efforts online will actually help you build your email list, your following and your business.

> "From the get-go I knew I had to have a strategy for each social network I put time and energy into. So many people share the same content on every network, which I think is a huge mistake since they are each so different.
>
> "Facebook has allowed me to engage in deep conversations, debates, and get real-time feedback from my audience. YouTube helps me put a personality to my brand, and it has helped me rank higher in search engines for relevant keywords in my niche. Then there's Twitter, which to this day has still been the best opportunity driver for my business and contributed more press to my business than any other platform, agency, or publicist."
>
> ~ *Natalie MacNeil, She Takes On The World*

Here's a step-by step strategy you can follow yourself:

These are the most common questions I get asked all the time. From this list you can build your own strategy using my free, downloadable template once you've set your goals and objectives (template available at **suitcaseentrepreneur.com/book/resources** under Chapter 8).

#1: What are the social media best practices?

- Treat Social Media like an offline relationship – don't sell right out of the gate, instead build up the friendship first

- Be LARGE — Listen, Ask, Respond, Give, Engage above all else

- Go for AAA – Be Authoritative + Authentic + Available

- Be consistent with your brand message (look and feel) across all sites

- Use a 1:10 ratio of selling vs sharing information wherever possible.

#2: How do I measure social media ROI?

- Measure what matters. Only measure those things that are related to your goals. Pick a few key things rather than trying to measure everything

- Set realistic goals like 200 new Facebook fans in 3 months accounting for 20% of visits to your website

- Track and measure actual reach and your conversation share (see my section later in this chapter on exactly how to this)

- Judge your success based on the number of recommendations and referrals you receive from the platforms you're engaging on.

#3: How do I best manage my time online?

- Spend 30-60 minutes per day doing the right things like engaging, sharing knowledge, adding value and answering questions

- Check-in 2-3 times per day to scan, engage & maintain interaction across your platforms (Hootsuite is my preferred tool for this)

- Focus on the top 3-5 tools and forget the rest. This will allow you to really master them and get results. You can add more sites later

- Set a weekly schedule and stick to it by actually blocking out time in your calendar and treating it as marketing, sales and customer service time

- Track your results and measure what's working on a regular basis (for me this is every two weeks) and then tweak your strategy based on results.

#4: How do I reach my target markets?

Do your due diligence and research on the audience demographics of the platforms you are on. Facebook, for example, has a large audience of women aged 55+ and LinkedIn is popular with executives over 30 earning $100K p.a.

Set up Google Alerts for your target market keywords, your business and your competition, so that you can keep track of what's hot, topical and where this is happening online.

Monitor who is talking (using the tools I mention next) and where they hang out. Then start engaging on those blogs, websites and forums.

Leave intelligent comments, opinions and links back to your own website so that you have a way of tracking whether this is working.

#5: How do I generate traffic and leads?

- State what value you provide & what problems you solve across all your social media sites. Do this in the copy you use on landing pages, in descriptions and in the consistent branding imagery you use on those same profiles. See examples of this on my Google Plus account, Facebook Page, YouTube Channel and Twitter profiles and notice how it's the same as on my website

- Provide links back to your website from the social media site you use, not just your main website URL but to other social media sites you frequently use

- Create calls-to-action on your own website: sign up, download, phone, register and subscribe. This builds a tribe you can communicate with regularly

- Establish a CRM system to ensure you capture leads. Use a service like Aweber, Mailchimp or InfusionSoft. Create separate lists based on your followers' interests: information gained from your calls-to-action

- Create specific content on your blog and in follow-up emails to convert these people into happy customers. If they signed up to download your social media book, then follow up in an email, telling them about your customized services or products, once you've established rapport with them and found out what they need.

The information above should give you a concrete start on how to focus on realistic goals for using social media on your own terms. From here you need to set objectives and a weekly action plan to get results.

Head to **suitcaseentrepreneur.com/book/resources** to download my free Social Media Strategy Template and get started today.

Tracking and monitoring social media mentions to optimize your strategy

Once you have your strategy in place, how do you know that it's working? You need to monitor how and where people are talking about you and your business. There is no one tool that does it all when it comes to aggregating and curating all social media mentions, but pick your favorites from the list below to make smart decisions about what you're doing well online.

Combine these results with your Google Analytics results to understand where your website and blog visitors are coming from and which pages and content are most popular. From there you can optimize your time spent on social media to give your brand and business the most leverage.

Tools to track your social media mentions and brand awareness

- **Hootsuite** is my social media dashboard of choice. You can track and monitor all mentions of all your social media profiles including Twitter accounts, Facebook pages and groups, LinkedIn, YouTube, Google Plus and more. You can post updates to multiple profiles in one click, set up streams to track keywords and hashtags and respond to all mentions and DMs plus track analytics on click-throughs.

- **Google Alerts** is a free service that allows you to enter relevant keywords or phrases you're interested in. Set one up for your name, your company, your competitors and industry topics, to get a daily email digest or as it happens' update on what's happening on the web.

- **Viralheat** covers every corner of the social web from Facebook, Twitter, Real-time web, to YouTube and lets you know your social media mentions.

- **Klout** shows how influential you are across the social networks and gives you an aggregate score of how much clout you have in your area of expertise (based upon your fans and followers), compared to others. It's a subjective but useful guide if you're into winning the popularity stakes.

The key is to track mentions and then take action

It's all about daily check-ins. My personal tip is to scan, engage and maintain in twenty minute chunks:

1. Respond to mentions in a timely manner and like a real person. Thank people for commenting or sharing. Start a conversation and ask them questions.

2. Point them to the right URL on your website or blog, or to the resource they're looking for, or to your contact page or the recent post they're referring to.

Next strategic steps to take

If what you're doing currently is working to build your community, your online brand presence and buzz, then keep doing more of it. By tracking and monitoring you will have a better understanding about which parts of social media are benefiting your business.

Now feed this into your ongoing marketing strategy. For example, in your Google Analytics metrics you notice a number of visitors and leads coming from Twitter and LinkedIn, but less from Facebook. What do you do?

- Look to enhance what you're doing on Twitter and LinkedIn and keep that as a key part of your marketing and engagement strategy.

- Look at what activities you did that week – which of your tweets were shared the most, which blog posts resonated most, which group discussions received the most comments? Note down what was most popular so that you can replicate this each week.

- See if you can improve the reach that your Facebook page is giving you. Run more competitions, post better content, ask questions, post videos or photos and see what is receiving more attention.

- Try Facebook advertising or sponsored stories for 2-3 weeks to see if you attract the right likes. If you haven't already, install a customized landing tab with a clear call-to-action, like joining your newsletter. This allows you to track whether Facebook is an effective lead generator for you.

Social media can be fun and profitable once you know how to approach it. Done right, it should be a joy, not a chore. More importantly, it should work together with the online systems you've set up and the business model you've created to work as your marketing, sales and customer service department 24/7.

Your social media homework

- Take time to apply all you've learned in this chapter and take 60 minutes to research the best platforms for your needs

- Once you've decided on the best platforms spend another hour or two updating your profile and information to present your brand well

- Reach out and connect with current customers and those who've referred you and ask for testimonials. Return the favor to them too

- Check your Google Analytics results and dig into what's driving your traffic and leads, then optimize that and stop doing the other stuff

- Download and fill out the Strategic Plan template (you'll find it at **suitcaseentrepreneur.com/book/resources** Chapter 8) and then take time to implement your strategies on a weekly basis as part of your schedule

- Come hang with me on Twitter @suitcasepreneur or connect with me on Facebook or Google Plus as a start.

Chapter 9

How to build a world-class team you may never meet.

The main ingredient of stardom is the rest of the team
~ JOHN WOODEN

I t's a common trait of entrepreneurs to want to do everything themselves, even when their business is outgrowing them. I mean, who else in the world can do your job better than you, right?

The truth is that there are thousands, if not hundreds of thousands, of talented freelancers and contractors out there who can often do the job better and usually for a fraction of the price and in half the time.

In your business, do you:

- Need a web developer or designer to deal with your website and graphics?

- Want a Google AdWords expert or SEO specialist to drive more traffic to your site?

- Need an affiliate marketing expert to manage your program?

- Want someone to deal with your email and calendar, that you're sick and tired of handling?

Outsourcing is the key and, frankly, I'm baffled as to why more small business owners, or even large firms, are not taking advantage of it. If you truly want to build a location independent business, then outsourcing is going to be your savior.

In this chapter you'll learn:

• Three reasons why most people don't delegate

• How to build a virtual team from scratch

• What to hand over and when

• Growing your team and hiring strategically

• Recognizing your team gaps

• A step-by-step guide to outsourcing your first job

Three reasons why you don't delegate

From personal experience and from talking to many entrepreneurs and clients, I've identified three key reasons why people don't delegate:

1. Our inner "control freak" and perfectionist tendencies mean we don't think anyone else can do the job better than we can.

2. We're usually running on a minimal budget and don't think we can afford to hire really talented people to whom we can delegate work.

3. We don't yet know how to go about hiring the right person and we have limited time to train new team members enough to trust them with the important work we desperately need done.

If you believe that any of the above statements are true, then you should know that they are all just excuses for not taking action.

You're not alone in your way of thinking, but you HAVE to change or you will not be able to grow your business or free up more time. Worse still, you will likely head towards burnout and I don't want that to happen to you.

If you're still not a believer, look at this great example of how you can make money outsourcing an entire product or part of your business.

"I outsourced my first iPhone app for $1,900. I had to post a job on Elance, and go through all the replies I got. I talked to a few of the candidates in more detail as I wanted to find the best fit for me, and the app I wanted to create. I settled on a team that wasn't the cheapest but also not the most expensive.

"I felt they could create the vision I had for my app. It took 7 months from start to finish, and when it was released, I made my money back in less than two weeks. It got picked up by Apple and was featured on the App storefront page for three weeks in a row.

"The first 30 days, I sold $30,000 worth of my 99c app. This was the first time I had outsourced anything that big! I took a risk and it paid off."

~ Benny Hsu

How to build a virtual team from scratch

I have built my team quite slowly but surely. The first hire is always the hardest, but trust me, it gets easier from there. For me, my first hire was my GVA — General Virtual Assistant. Even if you don't think you have the budget to hire someone, or you're not prepared to give over control, hiring a GVA will be the best decision you make for your business.

"I hired my GVA before I felt "ready" and I can honestly say that it was one of the most important decisions I made in the first year of my business. It's allowed me to do and try so many other things (revenue generating things!) because I am not focused on admin stuff. Well worth the money."

~ Jules Taggart

A full-time GVA will set you back around US$400 a month and prices go up depending on the level of experience and skill. I found mine through a referral. Margaret is a complete gem and is happy to do the work that I throw at her, as well as regular operational tasks. The extra time I now have has allowed me to focus on my "zone of genius" as well as playing more Ultimate Frisbee!

She works around 10-12 hours per week, based upon the amount of work I have for her, which includes tracking metrics twice a month, optimizing blog posts, scheduling calendar appointments, dealing with affiliate account setups and promotions, as well as responding to general inquiries through my contact form.

I hired her through Elance, so she simply logs her hours and uses their screenshot software to track what she's working on when. Each week Elance automatically bills my credit card and sends me an invoice and timesheet breakdown. I use this to see how long tasks have been taking her and adjust her workload where necessary.

Margaret is based in India and has excellent English. Her time-zone is handy as one of us is always working on something. I often wake up to find work she's done during my night, especially when I'm in the Northern hemisphere.

What to hand over and when:

For those of you reading this and wondering where to start, know that you are responsible for choosing how you spend your time. Once you realize how precious this is, and when you get comfortable delegating tasks you thought "only you could do", outsourcing starts to get addictive.

You realize you've been a fool for way too long, trying to write your newsletter, edit your blog posts, tweak audios and video, create all your content as well as managing your appointments, email and PR.

Here's an example in action:

> "I have been working with my grandson on a book for kids newly diagnosed with Type 1 diabetes and we were doing everything in the family, but the last steps just weren't happening, so I took my own advice.
>
> "I posted on Elance for an illustrator, then a fundraiser, then translators and proofreaders/editors. I have been deluged with amazing people who are not only good at what they do, but so many who are just good people, who want to help and go above and beyond any job description. It has helped to open the scope of our project beyond anyone's wildest imagination, all thanks to outsourcing!"
>
> *~ Randi Winter*

Start out small with your most repetitive tasks:

The first tasks you should delegate are the ones that can be easily systemized and currently take up too much of your time. Start with simple tasks that are important but not critical. Too often we become blind to what is really critical and what's not. Your life will not be destroyed if your newsletter goes out containing a small grammatical mistake.

For example, I used to spend 30-60 minutes optimizing and formatting each blog post I'd written and putting in photos so that it looked just perfect. Now Margaret does all this and she does it exactly as I would have done.

She progressed to helping with formatting my newsletter, cleaning up my email lists, handling changes in members' details from my programs, and updating key contacts in my CRM system. She also manages customer service for simple things like a download or template that got lost or a digital product that wasn't received.

Standard operating procedures

We work together using Standard Operating Procedures (SOPs), which are key to delegating work so that it still gets done just as I would have done it, or better. SOPs are basically written, step-by-step instructions to systemize each task into a process. Here's how:

1. Start a new document (Google Drive is easiest)

2. Give it an appropriate title, e.g. Responding to Contact Form Emails

3. When you next do this task write up the step-by-step process you take

4. Insert screenshots or video training where necessary to make it clearer

5. Insert exact wording to use or logic to follow, based on the email

6. Have your team member read through your SOP and do the task

7. Have them update the document instructions in their own words where something was not clear

8. Have them keep this document up to date for future team members too

9. Store this online or in your Dropbox folder under the SOP folder.

Here's an example in action:

I saved a massive amount of time when I handed over the growing volume of repetitive contact queries that I got through my website. Typically these fell into three categories:

• guest post or advertising requests

• selling services or products

• asking me for an interview or resources.

I wrote up templates for each of these common situations. Then I asked Margaret to install one of my favorite tools, Gmail Canned Responses. It saves a written response that can then simply be inserted into a new email. She saves more time now too and is more productive.

Top Tip: Take 10 minutes now to create short instructions for your GVA. Pick one of your most repetitive, time-sucking tasks that you deal with on a daily basis.

The easiest way is to make a short 'How-To' video using Jing or MeetingBurner. You can then have this transcribed into a word document by your GVA (and written up in their own words).

Make sure that they include a link to the video stored on Dropbox or as an unlisted YouTube Video for reference.

Keep these 'How-To' documents stored in a central folder that you share with your GVA and team on Dropbox so that the latest file is always accessible.

Growing your team

Hiring Margaret was vital before I headed off on the ride of my life across Africa for two months. I had done as much pre-content creation and scheduling and client handover before I left. But I knew I needed someone overseeing the day-to-day interactions, emails and social media updates.

The next hire I made was a WordPress expert. While I consider myself tech savvy, screwing around with code and tweaks on my website and blog is just not something I need to be doing – and nor should you.

He was another referral, this time from the lovely Amy Clover who is a former coaching client. She had raved about Alejandro (Alex) based in Mexico. I sent him an email and loved his super positive response on how he'd love to work with me and make my business shine.

To this day he's been one of the greatest supporters of my work and he makes any project I throw at him sound like the best thing on earth. He's on a monthly retainer and does unlimited changes and updates and tweaks to my site every month. These include optimizing my online shop, creating and updating landing pages, installing plugins, monitoring my site speed and fixing bugs.

His turnaround time is usually 24-48 hours and for more complex stuff I give him a lot of lead-time and heads up. This has freed up an unbelievable amount of time in my day and also allows me to access his knowledge with questions I have, or questions my clients may have too.

Top tip: Use a simple free project management tool like Asana to log tasks and due dates. Assign the tasks to your team members and include a short comment where more explanation is needed.

You receive email notifications on any tasks that are completed or due to be done. You can reply back via email and it's recorded on Asana directly.

Set up Asana to put your to-do tasks in your calendar so that you can see what you have to achieve. Ask your GVA or team members to do the same too.

Hiring strategically

After you've delegated your repetitive tasks and have outsourced the most time-consuming work to experts,what else can you hand over?

For me, my next hire was a podcast editor. Once again this was a referral, thanks to Jaime Tardy who has her own podcast. She highly recommended her editor Rolly, based in the Philippines, so long as I didn't steal all his time away.

I've hired him via oDesk, so once again I get billed only for the amount of work he does, for which I pay through PayPal. I was quick to realize that editing audio was a complete drag to me. My skills are in interviewing my guests and that's where my time is best spent.

Now I simply record my podcasts on Skype, using Call Recorder to capture the MP3. I then copy this file into my dedicated Dropbox folder for podcasts that Rolly has access to and he receives a notification that it's there.

I record my short 5-10 second intros on my iPhone (yes really) or Camtasia and and email Rolly the file direct. He works his magic and puts it in the "Ready For Upload" file. As you can see, this is not a fancy setup – just flexible, on-the-go methods that work for traveling entrepreneurs.

He works around eight hours per month for me and edits multiple podcast sessions at a time, as I usually get several done in advance for bulk editing. He's also highly responsive. Once again this is the beauty of working with virtual teams based in other time-zones.

I even handed over the blog write-ups for each episode and the podcast publishing and syndication to my team member Cher, simply by following the Podcast SOP of exactly how this should all be handled. This has saved me hours each week.

I then extended this same strategy to my videos. I hired a videographer while in Berlin to shoot 15 videos in a row with me that answered my readers' questions on business, travel and lifestyle.

Then, thanks to a friend's referral, I hired my first video editor Tim, based in the Netherlands. Even though I personally enjoy the editing process, it's very time consuming and I felt it was about time I had an expert do this.

Tim edits several of my videos at a time, and then Cher takes over to do the write up and formatting, before I sign off on the finished production and post.

Recognizing your team gaps

I highly recommend you put together an Organizational Chart for your business (hat tip to the lovely Systems Business Coach founder Beverlee Rasmussen for showing me this tool many years back). Although I had seen it in the corporate world, I had never thought to apply it to my small business.

Even though you might be a solopreneur, that doesn't mean that you can't start to think of your future, full-grown company and of filling the various roles, so that you can remove yourself from them as you grow and scale your business. Typically you keep yourself as the CEO or Chief Adventurer as I've labeled myself and then you start to hire to fill the rest, bit by bit.

It works best if you hire someone to cover your most pressing need, based on your business expansion plans for growth. It's up to you to decide whether you want permanent full time or part-time staff or freelance contractors. I'd suggest that a combination works best.

So how did I find my most important hire, Cher? She is my Chief Happiness Officer and Online Business Manager and I've trained and mentored her in this role so that she is continually stepping up to own it.

Cher came to me through my $100 Change Program, where she was on my early access email list. One day she replied to an email, volunteering to help me out, as she so loved the concept and what I did.

> **Top tip:** If you're doing work that inspires people and gets noticed, you will definitely find people want to be a part of your team. Often the right person to hire is already within your friend or business network, or community. Reach out and ask for referrals or for people who are interested in the role you have on offer. You'll often find you hire people who are your biggest advocates and already understand why you do what you do and your business ethos.

Online business manager

One role that is relatively new, that has grown from the online nature of many businesses, is the Online Business Manager. Depending upon the type of business you intend to build, this role is like your right hand operational and strategic sidekick.

As Tina Forsyth, author of Becoming an Online Business Manager' and The Entrepreneur's Trap puts it:

"Most business owners look to hire an Online Business Manager (OBM) when they simply cannot grow their business anymore being the only one in charge. In order for them to take their business to the next level they need to pull themselves out of the day-to-day management activities and focus on growth like product development, strategic alliances and big picture business planning. Everything else becomes the responsibility of the OBM – a virtually based support professional who manages your online businesses, including the day-to-day management of projects, operations, team members and metrics."

After interviewing Cher about her core strengths and skill set and conducting some psychometric tests like Myers Briggs, I realized that she was a great fit for helping with the top-level strategy for my business as well as the operational side.

This includes jobs such as evaluating speaking opportunities, streamlining my business processes, building out content for upcoming product launches, as well as editing our self-publishing efforts. We Skype every week and go over the business growth plans and most important actions that need tackling.

Top tip: Video calls and regular team meetings on Skype or Google Hangouts do a great job of keeping communication lines clear and everyone on the same track. However, there's nothing like being able to meet in person to build a better bond when the opportunity comes around. I've met up with Cher on a hillside villa in Naples, Italy and London, England for strategic planning sessions, and in the Portland and Las Vegas in USA.

Like the rest of my small, but efficient team, Cher is somebody I trust completely. She's based in the US, and communicates just like I do, which is something I really value. She's hungry to learn about online marketing, affiliates, ecommerce and building an online business, as she builds her own.

I pay her a monthly retainer that will increase as her role's responsibilities and breadth grow. The more money I make in my business, the more I can invest into my team, expanding it so that I can hand over more of my work, in turn allowing me to reach a broader audience around the world.

What types of jobs can you outsource?

What do you not enjoy doing? What's taking up most of your time and is not critical for you to do? It's easiest when you look at your business needs and the gaps that need to be filled.

Some areas to consider are:

- Online Business Management

- Marketing and Sales

- Strategy, planning and mentoring support

- Administrative support

- Financial management

- Design and branding support

- Tech and development support.

A step by step guide to outsourcing

I want to give you a clear step-by-step example of how you can start out with a small task to test the waters of outsourcing. I know it can be scary, but realize how much more effective you'll be when you can focus on using your key strengths and outsource the rest.

Don't think that handing over control and tasks to other people means that they'll steal your intellectual property or run off with your passwords. In this day and age, freelancers are in abundance and they're used to working with online tools and systems to manage your work and that of their clients. Plus you can refer to the tools I outline in Chapter 13 to protect your online assets, especially while traveling.

I've seen people outsource pretty crazy things. Taki Moore has outsourced his email entirely and never deals with it anymore. He used SOPs to deal with every single type of email that came in and create appropriate responses. Now he focuses on training other coaches via Skype and in-person to build their businesses.

Others outsource their life, including having their GVAs book their travel, organize their dry cleaning and make their doctor's appointments. The sky is the limit. Open your mind to what you can effectively delegate that you really don't need to be doing.

An outsourcing case study in action

Back when I first started my blog, I wanted to understand what the competition was doing, who I could emulate and how I could set myself apart. But I was still full-time co-founder at ConnectionPoint Systems Inc. and did not have the time to research hundreds of sites, get their contact details and make summary notes. So I outsourced it on oDesk. Here's how you can do the same:

1. Create the job

Write up a few, short paragraphs of job description, specifically outlining what you need. Keep this in a document for future use.

2. Create the account

Set up a new account on oDesk and link your payment source to a credit card (you can use PayPal and direct debit too).

3. Post the job

Select "Post a new job", select the right category and cut and paste in the job description. Specify under skills the language that you want them to be proficient in and three or four specific skills you believe they must have. In my case these were "Market Research" and "MS Excel".

4. Publish the job

Set the amount you're willing to pay per hour or for the whole contract. In this case it was a budget of $20 for 3 hours.

5. Select your candidate

If it's a fairly straightforward job you will probably receive applications within minutes, since oDesk has over 1 million within its freelancing community. Delete the standard responses so that you can deal with someone who cares enough to provide a personal response and state their relevant experience. Check if their skills fit with what you required.

> **Top tip:** Do not spend hours going through every single application. You will start to judge for yourself whether this hourly bid is too low, or you can often judge from their profile picture and title whether they're the right fit, or just mass applying for any job.

6. Making the hire

Hire two people (especially if they're within budget) for a simple task or for a relatively short-term contract. Send them the same task and judge them side-by-side. If one doesn't work out you can terminate their contract with one click. The other hire will still be working on the job at hand.

7. Get the job done

When you select 'Hire this person', attach a short job description with the project parameters they are to follow and report back on, plus a deadline. The deadline is the most important factor. Better yet, use your SOP for them to follow step by step.

The result of my experiment

Twenty-four hours later both contractors had sent me in-depth excel spreadsheets with competitor research that had taken them under 5 hours each and had cost me a grand total of US $16. Yep, you can do the math. This was dirt cheap and ridiculously useful.

It was far more practical than if I'd done the work using my hourly rate. Plus I don't like doing research at the best of times. My strength lies in pulling meaning out of the results. I got the info I needed in a quick turnaround time and went on to use both hires to do further work for me.

What sites are the best for outsourcing?

As the virtual work team has taken off, so too has the plethora of cool sites and services to help you find your ideal candidate. Below I've collated the ones that come most recommended, several of which I use personally.

Elance, like oDesk, has a huge community of freelance workers. It allows you to post a job and review candidates. You can track your projects and the hours worked, plus you can also pay by credit card or PayPal and set up automatic billing so that you don't need to manually pay your team.

> "I used outsourcing for video editing for my online resource center to support my book. I required editing and reformatting of 17 videos all between 3 and 5 minutes long. I used Elance, made my request as specific as possible, looked at respondents and picked a guy in Holland who had good reviews.
>
> He was quick and went waaaay beyond the brief. I ended up paying him an additional $50 as a bonus, but it was well worth it. The whole job only ended up costing $150, which I think was a bargain for what he did, and the quality of his work. I have recommended him to others and will definitely use him again in the future."
>
> ~ *Kirsten Hodgson*

Virtual Staff Finder

If you are struggling to make a hire and don't want to do the work yourself, then I highly recommend checking out my friend Chris Ducker's Virtual Staff Finder service, where they will source and interview your perfect new candidate. You then you hire the candidate on your own terms and using agreed upon rates.

"I outsourced customer service to a full-time employee in the Philippines that costs us US$450 a month. Here's how:

1. Hired through Virtual Staff Finder

2. Set up a Zendesk account to capture and log customer enquiries and issues

3. Created templates and procedures to follow (new procedures are created by the employee as needed)

4. Customer service tickets get handled daily

"The results are very positive. Rarely do I have to think about customer service. It frees up a huge amount of mental bandwidth. In my opinion customer service is one of the first things to get off your plate, IMO if your company has regular product sales."

~ *Jason Van Orden*

Hire My Mom

Hiremymom.com is a popular site, particularly for those wanting office managers and assistants who are trustworthy. Their community comprises stay-at-home mums to a large extent. These are often top personal assistants and executives who no longer want to work full time, or prefer to work on their own terms.

99 Designs and Crowdspring

You can turn to 99designs and Crowdspring for specific design work like websites, logos and branding. These sites are great as you pay a one-off set fee and people bid for your project by actually showing you their designs for your proposal.

Fiverr

If you're on a really tight budget, check out fiverr.com where you can find a community of freelancers willing to do just about anything for $5. Generally you get what you pay for, but it's just the start to finding someone talented to hire on a longer term at his real rates.

Mechanical Turk

Mechanicalturk is a service provided by Amazon, which is great for entrepreneurs and developers who need small "human intelligence tasks" done like writing a product description in another language or choosing the best photos for a website. It's a large-scale workplace community where you can hire someone for even a single task.

Microtask

Microtask is a platform for real-time and scalable on-demand outsourcing. They have built a fancy platform that divides assignments into small tasks, distributes them to an online workforce around the world and collects the results. They operate on a pay-as-you-go pricing model.

Putting it all together

As you can see, no empire was built over night, so don't feel you have to get it right from the very beginning. But there's also nothing stopping you from starting today. Make sure you build your team one step at a time. With each step give more control and responsibility over to your team, and become a better leader yourself. You will see yourself implementing better systems and improving inefficiencies in your own processes and your business will improve as a result.

For me, it has been about painting a clear vision of where I want my business to go and then bringing my team onboard with that. I have written my

5-page "painted picture" of where I want my business to be in 3 years' time (hat tip to Cameron Herold from his book Double Double).

I turned my vision into a Slideshare presentation, to publicly share it with the world, and it continues to receive thousands of views. See it for yourself: How to Create Freedom in Business.

Create your own vision for your business. This will make you work towards ensuring your business gets to where you want it to go, towards the future and the lifestyle you've envisioned for yourself, until it becomes a reality. Have your team read and refer to it regularly too, to make sure everyone has a clear sense of what you're building together.

Making your first hire, or even your fourth or fifth is a lot easier when you have your vision pinned down for your business, with a clear idea of what areas need the most help right now. From there, it's about prioritizing your hires, and building a great team of talented people who are smarter than you are. That's when you start to see real business growth and realize that you don't have to do it all by yourself.

Your homework to get more freedom:

- Head to **suitcaseentrepreneur.com/book/resources** to watch my video interview with Chris Ducker on how to become an outsourcing expert and build a virtual team

- Create your own Organizational Chart and identify the key gaps you'd like to fill within the next 3 months

- Use the step-by-step guide to making your first outsourcing hire in this chapter by posting a job today, on one of the recommended sites above, and test out a task or project you're comfortable with delegating.

Act 3

How on earth does one become a Suitcase Entrepreneur?

"The world is a book and those who do not travel read only one page."
~ ST AUGUSTINE

You'd think that packing up your life into a bag or two would make everything that much more simple. In many ways it does. But then you're faced with the great problem of too many choices.

Where should you travel? How long should you go for? What is the purpose of your journey? Can you really work from anywhere?

In the following chapters I cover whether you're actually cut out to be a homeless vagabond, or whether a variation of living and working from anywhere will suit you best.

Then we dive into the tools and technology to make your travels that much more effortless as well as the travel hacking tips you can put to use to go places for free, and much more.

"In 2001, on a flight from Miami to LA where a passenger passed away, I had the idea to launch a drink to help people fly well. It took me another 6 years and 3 passports worth of travel to act. The only regret I have now (5 years on from acting) is that I didn't act sooner.

I'd been 'sold up the creek' that I needed the great role, the money, the lifestyle and that leaving my corporate job was risky. And a lot of people were selling me on that; my boss, my colleagues, friends, the media, but mainly my own ego and the last one was selling hard."

Stripped back to no salary and living of savings for two years and another business my wife started the enduring thoughts that entered my mind were:

1. What we really need in life is to be the author our own destinies and to help others — that makes us happy.

2. The only risk is waking up in 30-50 years time with no magical stories of journeys taken and mountains conquered.

Natalie didn't have this all worked out from day one. She began. She purchased a ticket. She hopped on the plane determined to author her own destiny, to live a life full of magical journeys and mountains conquered.

Its great to have people like her passing on their experience and inspiring more to act because we were born to explore. Selfishly it makes us better people, but unselfishly it leads to a better world. And in this day and age, when we can work from just about anywhere, why wouldn't you begin as soon as possible?"

Roger Boyd, founder of 1Above, the Flight Drink and generous sponsor of Act 3.

Chapter 10

How to become a pro at being homeless.

When you set out on an adventure, all kinds of unexpected things can happen. You don't always know where you'll end up, and your adventure will likely contain a certain amount of risk. But as I learned to accept monotony as a traveler's friend, I know I must also welcome the element of uncertainty on the road to adventure.

~ CHRIS GUILLEBEAU

I meet people every day that tell me I'm 'living the dream' when they find out what I do, or that I've created 'the dream job'. While I admit there's nothing else I'd rather be doing, this way of life is not for everyone, and sometimes too much freedom can be tough to deal with.

Perhaps you're longing to grab your laptop and take off somewhere exotic, packing up all your stuff and going down the minimalist route, like I have. Or you might simply want to enjoy greater flexibility and work from home and cosy cafes.

Whatever your ideal lifestyle looks like, you need to know it's a whole new ball game when you combine it with running a business at the same.

In this chapter you'll learn:

- The key characteristics you need to succeed at this lifestyle

- The pros and cons of being a suitcase entrepreneur

- How to make the most of your unconventional lifestyle

- How to stay fit and healthy on the road

- How to create lasting friendships and relationships on the move

Are you suited to this lifestyle?

This is an important question to ask before you set off on your journey. People tend to glamorize this lifestyle and forget about what it really takes to live your dream.

There's a price to pay for freedom, and it often comes in the form of other people, who might not understand your choices, or who resent your seemingly perfect lifestyle. This means, that in addition to staying true to leading a life where you prioritize what's important to you, you'll also have to think about others.

This comes with the territory when you choose to go against societal norms. And it's not going to be easy, But then again, who wants easy when you can have life full of adventure?

But … it's not always fun to sit in airports, go on long train journeys, be in noisy cafes with dodgy Internet or pack up your suitcase for the umpteenth time. It can get lonely on the road, too.

Still, it's important that you know what you're signing up for to lead this Suitcase Entrepreneur lifestyle (and that of an entrepreneur in general), so take a look at this list below and see if it's a really a good fit for you:

Key qualities and characteristics you need

- A vision for your business and life that you will fight for

- A strong sense of purpose and what's important to you

- Determination, persistence and the ability to hustle

- Living your dream no matter what other people think

- The ability to spend time alone and enjoy your own company

- An independent nature and strength of character to deal with daily challenges

- A fearless attitude to travel and business (or at least the ability to push past your fears)

- Decision making and planning capabilities you can continue to build on, and discipline you can act on

- A desire to explore and experience new places

- An open mind and sense of compassion for others.

All that might seem like a lot, and you may not tick the box on every count, but acknowledging your strengths and weaknesses at this stage will really help you in the long run. This is truly the time you get to put those limiting beliefs aside and consider how important living life on your own terms really is to you.

"My nomadtopia happens to be with an entire family, multiple pets and a 40 foot container. We all set our own rules and if what you experienced previously didn't turn out to be your ideal, keep trying. What you want at a certain age will change the next year and the year after. The point is that you can change your mind on what your ideal life should look like. Relish your experiences. Keep going!"

~ *Cheryl Bigus*

The pros and cons of being a Suitcase Entrepreneur

When I thought about all the things I love about leading a minimalist lifestyle, like being constantly on the move and having no fixed abode, I realized these unique aspects can also be the downsides that make it so unappealing to others.

I'll never forget the day, after years of hearing people say 'Oh I'd love to be able travel the world, doing what I love' I had someone tell me the complete opposite. She wrote an email to me wondering how on earth I could stand living out of a suitcase and have no real home.

It took me by surprise to think people thought like this, but as the years have gone on, I can definitely say there are moments, when I'm packing my suitcase yet again, when I'd rather just stay put.

Below you'll find the broader advantages and disadvantages, which should give you a taste of what you'll encounter.

Important: I've based this list on leading a life where you are traveling regularly and running a full time business.

Pros	Cons
Freedom to work anywhere	No set place to work from
No need to sit in commuter traffic wasting precious hours	Figuring out where you're going to work each day
Freedom to choose what hours you want to work that suit you	Lack of routine or set working hours
Making your own decision about what to work on each day	Having to make all the decisions about what you'll work on
Choosing who you work with and having no virtual geographic boundaries	Dealing with multiple time zones and not meeting people face to face as often
Being able to run your entire business using your laptop, smartphone and Internet and online tools	Relying on technology for almost everything and dealing with the frustrations when it does not work when you need it most
Creating your own revenue streams, products and services	Relying on yourself (and your team) to create your success
Knowing you are in charge of your unlimited earning potential	Being responsible for creating your own financial security
Freedom to make decisions on every aspect of your life and business to fit with your priorities	Dealing with the constant challenge of changing location and planning every aspect of your life and travel
Living minimally and feeling free from the weight of possessions (both mentally and physically) so you can move around quickly and with ease	Not having the creature comforts that make you feel at home, or being able to have everything at your finger tips for every occasion
Choosing when and where you want to take time off and for how long	Creating a balance between disconnecting from your work and enjoying your travels
Creating new connections and making new friends on the road while exploring new countries and cultures.	Not being able to spend quality time with your friends and family or rely on your local support network.

If you're not put off by the cons then you're most definitely suited to a life of freedom in business and travel.

The unexpected travelers education

Travel is one of the few things that teaches you life skills you won't find in any university. It teaches you that you're not invincible, things aren't always as they seem, that you can't always stay in control and that you should expect the unexpected.

I like it because you learn how to make quick decisions acting on limited (and sometimes dubious) information or others' opinions. You learn how to manage multiple projects like planning your journey, packing your life up, and dealing with last minute changes like a pro. You can then apply this in business to your advantage.

If you want creature comforts and familiarity, then I suggest you stay at home. Here's an example from my journey that highlights why it's so important to know what your traveler profile really is:

When I was on Borneo Island, I decided to stay in a Longhouse, on a remote organic farm to write this book. It had basic amenities, windows with no glass, slat floorboards and a river running underneath it. Each day would bring hot and humid sunshine followed by torrential downpours on the tin roof and thunderstorms that vibrated the earth beneath me. Ants dined at the table with me, geckos adorned my walls and mosquitos feasted on my legs and arms nightly.

I'd be privy to all sorts of strange and wonderful animal and bird calls high up in the trees on a daily basis. At night I'd listen as some strange object fell noisily on the roof or into the water. To me it was an experience in nature, and I got to share it with the nine dogs, many geese, goats, chickens, turkeys, pigeons and one cute but whiny cat.

I was there for over a week and made a firm friend with a girl from the US who enjoyed it as much as I did, and together we headed off for hikes, naked swims in waterfalls and visits to National parks. When she left, she was replaced by a German lady who hated practically everything I loved about the place. She complained day and night about everything that I hadn't even considered.

It struck me that she was in the wrong place for her level of travel comfort. She needed to stay in a place that had access to shops and transport, modern facilities and a superior standard of comfort. She cut her stay short (thankfully) and took herself off to another place. Rumor has it she had something to complain about there too.

I adore the lessons I've learned from traveling the world since I was a small kid in diapers. It makes you more well-rounded and, if you keep an open mind, it can diminish any racial or religious biases you may have had towards cultures before you were exposed to them.

Travel, even within your own country, lets you see humans for who they are, not their race, religion or color. You begin to understand how history has shaped who we are, how we act and why we live as we do. That beats any kind of education you can buy and it sets you up for a rich and varied set of life experiences. This, again, translates into your business dealings: you actually have a deeper understanding for your global customer base, and your tribe.

Choosing the right type of travel mode

When it comes to running your business and traveling the world, you have to figure out what level of location independence is going to suit you and make you most happy. As you saw in the real-life examples of entrepreneurs living and working on their own terms in Chapter 4, there's no cookie-cutter model that works best.

You can choose to base yourself in one location and take mini-adventures each month — either within your country or across continents. Or you could spend half a year snowboarding in the French Alps and the other half scuba diving in the South Pacific. Or maybe you want to change destinations every single week so you can see the entire world?

It's completely up to you, but take a look at the list of pros and cons again before you decide on what suits you best and consider the following:

- Are you good at managing your own time or do you need routine in your day to be productive?

- Do you work well on your own or do you crave interactions with people or need to see your friends regularly?

- Can you work from anywhere or do you require peace and quiet and a proper office or working space?

- Are you comfortable using online tools and technology and sitting behind a laptop for hours on end?

- Do you adjust well to constant time zone changes and can sleep well no matter what, or are you sensitive to environmental changes?

- Do you gain energy from being in summer climates or cool winters?

- Are you good at motivating yourself to eat well and stay fit no matter what or do you need a gym or sports group to stay active?

There are likely a ton of other questions I could ask you but hopefully this gives you an insight into what you need to consider.

"My hubby and I travelled east from the UK across Russia, China, Vietnam, Australia and Thailand, for our honeymoon. And while it was absolutely wonderful, I kinda wish we'd stopped after China. We were away for 14 months and by the time we reached Thailand, the novelty had well and truly worn off.

We had stopped marveling at temples, as we felt we'd seen it all before, and we were no longer wowed by gorgeous scenery. We stopped appreciating our wonderful amazing world.

It's ok to want to settle, to stop and be still. I strongly feel that to truly appreciate travelling, I have to stop and come home where it's normal and a little bit boring maybe. I have to reset back to normal to really be amazed by the un-normal.

~ *Kerry*

Personally, it's only taken me seven years of traveling the world and another three years of having no home to start to think that having a base is actually necessary to enjoy your nomadic lifestyle. The consensus is the same with many friends I speak to who've been on the road for 5-10 years doing the same.

There comes a point when you just want to leave your few possessions in a spot you can come back to, even just for a week. Be it a shed, a storage locker, a beach hut or a small inner city apartment, it gives you a sense of place and a base from which to explore more fully.

"I just spent a year traveling as a career break and experienced so much of what you describe and it made me never want to live the life of a nomad. On the other hand, it did show me that I would like to be location-independent. To me, that means having a home base with a job that allows me to come and go as I please. So if I want to jet off to Europe for a couple weeks, I can do so while working remotely, but I'll have a nice familiar bed and friends and routine waiting for me when I get back home."

~ *Katie Aune*

Making the most of your unconventional lifestyle

I get asked all the time how I stay focused on the road, how I deal with clients in different time zones and how I get so much done while traveling all the time. So here are the lessons I've learned from over three years of doing this full time.

1. Set a daily schedule

It's all very well having a business that gives you the all the freedom in the world to do what you want. But the flipside of this is knowing what to do with it, and how to manage it. You'll be faced with endless options to choose from in terms of where you can base yourself, what you want to work on, who you want to work with and how you want to spend your time off.

This may sound like a fun 'problem' to have, and on the whole it is, however I know many people who struggle with defining what living life on their own terms is and don't deal well with a lack of structure to their day to keep them in check. So here's what I recommend:

Your six step daily success plan:

1. **Identify your most important actions (MIAs)** at the beginning of your day, or the night before. This is the only list you look and focus on, until you've completed these priorities. These should align with your goals you've set for your business and life.

2. **Block out distraction-free time.** In order to focus on your MIA it's important to establish how your day will roll so you need to carve out blocks of time (20 minutes, 1 hour, 2 hours etc) that become your sacred work time. Disconnect from the internet, turn off your mobile and shut the door, or go and work in a park or café.

3. **Take regular breaks.** In between your blocks of time you've carved out you need to leave space to stop, stretch, dance, and get some fresh air. This actually makes you more productive and helps you focus back in on what you're doing. Five minutes is good for smaller blocks, and 30-60 minutes is great when you've been working longer.

4. **Limit the tasks you set yourself.** Outside of your MIAs you will naturally have several other small 'to-dos' so put them on a physical sticky note or use a simple tool like TeuxDeux. Limit these to no more than 5, and be realistic. Examples to include are 'Pay affiliates', 'Renew passport', 'Transfer photos to hard drive'. Any that you don't get done, transfer over to the next day.

5. **Stop multi-tasking. Start single-tasking.** Even though you're think you're being effective with seventeen browser tabs open, notifications turned on and instant messaging, you're probably not fully focusing on any one task. Practice mindfulness and concentrate fully. Use apps like Freedom for MAC or Leechblock Firefox extension to block out all distracting sites (especially social media) at set times in the day so you get real work done.

6. **Batch your tasks.** To make single tasking easier, it helps to put repetitive work into batches like a time to check and process your email, check in on social media, do your accounts, plan your editorial calendar and

scheduling calls with clients or friends. It's honestly best to do these later in the day when your energy is lower and your MIAs are complete.

2. Create balance and routine.

The biggest challenge if you're traveling regularly is keeping a sense of balance and routine in your life – and having both of those things is the key to real freedom. My number one tip to you is that the more disciplined you are, the more freedom you will have.

There's a reason people go into offices with set hours – it trains you to get into a routine. If you're not a naturally organized or disciplined person, then I advise you set up a daily routine that works for you. That may be getting up early to do yoga, and get your key work out of the way before 8am, followed by client work and then taking the rest of the day off to explore and relax.

Or it may mean that you do your best work between 11pm and 4am. Whatever works for you to make the most of the day – establish a routine, and then use my 6 Step Plan to schedule in your work. Then stick with it 80% of the time. Why 80%? Because we're all human and life will get in the way, despite your best intentions, especially when you're traveling. Watch my YouTube video on how to increase productivity in your business from anywhere that covers both your daily success plan and routine.

3. Set boundaries (but break them from time to time)

While many location independents claim to be living the dream, they're often working insane hours and find it hard to disconnect from the 24/7 online world, for even a few hours. This defeats the purpose of working on a beautiful island, if you never look up from your laptop, right? They have not set proper boundaries.

Once I got my business to a point where it didn't need me, then I was able to enjoy my travels even more. So even though I stick to my daily schedule and focus on a weekly routine that allows me to achieve my three-month business goals, building in flexibility is key.

> **Top Tip:** For me it's important to be present and enjoy every moment. That means I pack up my laptop and disconnect from the Internet whenever possible. I can focus on going on a jungle trek in Borneo, or a river cruise to see pygmy elephants, proboscis monkeys and orangutans. My work can wait until later.
>
> If I have a deadline for a project or a launch that requires me to focus then I'll happily book into a place for a week to put my head down and get it done. But I will always make time to go and explore during the day to ensure I'm living life to the full.

4. Keep up appearances and keep your clients:

One thing I've learned the hard way is that when you're working from the road (or the air or water) it can be pretty hard to keep your appointments. I've missed more meetings over the past few years then I care to admit, and often that's completely my fault due to a time zone screw up, or a miscommunication or packing in too much and not allowing enough time.

But sometimes it can come down to circumstances beyond your control, like a lack of Internet when you expected it most (this happened in Portugal before my coaching call, despite scoping out the venue and testing the Internet four hours before hand). Or a delayed flight, a missed train or a weather storm can stop you from reaching your location.

If you don't want to piss off your valued clients, customers and friends then I have four tips for you, particularly if you're in a service based business and rely on active streams of revenue from services like web design, speaking, coaching, or consulting.

1. **Clearly communicate with your clients.** Let them know in advance when you're going away, how best to contact you as well as when they can expect to hear back from you and to expect the unexpected. (I can't tell you how many missed appointments have happened due to Internet or transport delays but most of the time people are understanding, given the nature of my life and business).

2. **Control your time wisely.** Use an online scheduling service like Schedule Once to allow clients to book meetings online for convenient times you've blocked out, and which shows them the appointment in their own time zone.

3. **Promote your mobile lifestyle the right way.** Use a service like timeanddate.com to figure out your time zone differences and put these in your email auto-responder, out of office message or email signature for family, friends and networks to stay informed. Change your location on key sites like Skype, Facebook and Twitter so that geo-location updates are correct.

4. **Say no to extra commitments**. Especially if they don't align with what's your on your important list. That means saying no to a 'free advice session over coffee or via Skype', involvement on a project, going to an event, or reviewing a book or document for a friend. List and evaluate your commitments on a weekly basis and start saying "no" more frequently.

The best way to enjoy your travels and keep your clients happy is to compartmentalize your schedule to suit your own needs. For example, you could spend three months of the year doing all your coaching and consulting for clients in person, then block out the next three months to focus on travel, creative work or business development for the quarter ahead.

Staying fit and healthy on the road

Traveling the world doesn't mean you have to skimp on your health, but it does take a lot of extra effort and discipline to make time for it when you don't have a regular routine.

Traveling can also put an array of tempting and delicious foods in front of you on a daily basis that are too good to pass up. That leads you to you overindulge on rich foods and alcohol more often than normal. (That's part of the joy of traveling, if you ask me!)

Depending on the type of travel you have planned, you may well be doing more physical activity than normal if you're sightseeing or simply needing to walk everywhere. If you're an adventure trip then it's likely being active is a key part of your day too.

But if you're working and traveling consistently, staying fit and healthy is going to play a key part in keeping your energy levels up so you can be more productive, do and see more as well as run your business.

Six ways to add a daily dose of fitness into a busy schedule

1. Book accommodation that has a gym or swimming pool, or has a fitness center located nearby that you can visit.

2. Download Insanity workouts on to your laptop so you can do a 30 minute bodyweight workout in a 6ft by 6ft space or less.

3. Get a subscription to iYoga and put together your own customized mix of yoga poses so you can perform a 10 minute session on the go, or a longer one when you most need it.

4. Go for a run or walk to get familiar with the area you're staying and use it as a sightseeing experience at the same time.

5. Set that alarm clock 30 minutes earlier to get in your session, even on days you're traveling to the airport early — you'll feel refreshed and energized for the day ahead.

6. Skip that last client drink at the bar or make your dinners earlier so you can get adequate rest. Make a commitment to your health.

Watch my video on four ways to stay fit and healthy while traveling for extra tips and entertainment (you'll find the link at **suitcaseentrepreneur. com/resources** Chapter 10).

Go nuts on nutrition

Being on the move can make it difficult to stay healthy and make smart food choices, especially in some countries where 'vegetarian' is not a recognized word. So take back control and come prepared.

• Bring trail mix (nuts and dried fruits) along with you always. It's an ideal snack that satiates your appetite, keeps your energy up during meetings and gets you by in between meal services on long-haul flights

• Protein or energy bars are a useful alternative that have a long expiry date, and don't get you in trouble in countries that have strict customs rules and don't allow fruit and nuts.

• Instant porridge (oatmeal) is the bomb because all you need is a small Tupperware container to bring with you and a plastic spoon. Then you just need to mix it with hot water for a healthy, nutritious breakfast.

• Vitamin C tablets (especially those dissolvable in water) are a great anecdote to constant late nights and early starts as they give you an extra boost – they're also a great hangover cure.

• Bring your own tea bags so you don't end up drinking five cups of coffee per day. Make a concerted effort to fill yourself with herbal teas so that you remain clear and focused not wired and strung out.

- Pack a trusty Nalgene bottle – unbreakable, light and convenient, you can just keep filling them with water to stay hydrated on your travels.

How to make lasting friendships

I'm fortunate to have a large group of friends and family scattered around the world who I catch up with whenever I'm 'coming to a town near them', which is quite likely, given my travels. I've found that no matter how many months or years it's been, true friends will always pick up where we left off, just like old times.

It can be really hard to leave good, life-long friends behind. In fact many people return home because of homesickness. How do you keep close friends when you're far away?

Tips for keeping your friendships strong:

- **Touch base** with your closest friends via text messages, emails, post-cards or chats on social media sites to keep each other up to date on your news

- **Hang out** virtually with video sessions on Skype or Google Hangout or Facetime. There's a lot to be said for seeing someone's face. Communication is 90% visual. It makes you feel instantly more connected.

- **Engage with them**. Remember not to dominate the conversation with your amazing travel stories and worldly experiences. While your life may be exciting to you and make theirs pale in comparison, what they're doing in their daily lives is just as important to them.

- **Move on** if your friends are not adjusting well to your nomadic tendencies or find it hard to reconnect each time you're home or make it difficult for you to leave again. This may sound harsh but it's part of life. True friends will be with you in life no matter what. Other friends will come and go and for each person who you lose touch with, you'll meet plenty more on your travels.

How travel changes you

One thing you probably won't miss is being responsible to all those people back home, which can be a burden, no matter how much you love your friends and family or partner. Even if you like to feel like your part of a community, you likely won't miss the endless commitments to groups, clubs or committees you've joined over the years.

Once you're far away from home you get a better perspective on which relationships and connections no longer serve a purpose, or were even limiting you.

That's because travel is liberating. It allows you to leave all that behind and be free to be whoever you want. You also choose how you want to be seen by strangers because they don't know you from a bar of soap. In many ways it's a chance to reinvent yourself or focus on being the person you want to be.

"When you live in one place, you tend to have a group of friends, family and co-workers who know you as you know them. These people mean very well, but because they know you so well, they also treat you the way they expect you to be; if you're the class clown, you'll always be the class clown to them. It's incredibly difficult to change who you are or what you believe when everyone around you is treating you like the person you've always been.

"When you're on the road, however, you only have very limited contact with others, and that contact can be as frequent or infrequent as you want. If you want to think through your entire life philosophy and change everything about it, you can, and there's no one there to act as if it's weird or that you've changed...you can be whomever you want, and that allows you to evolve your mentality and philosophies quite rapidly.

"I LOVE this freedom, and it's probably the last thing I would ever give up, now that I've had it (and is a big part of why I don't know that I'll ever be able to totally rejoin society as I lived in it before I started traveling)."

~ *Colin Wright interview with Kent Healy*

If you find yourself in this position of having reinvented yourself, as many travelers do, then it is time for you to create a new circle of friends and entrepreneurs who "get you" and that will come on your new journey with you.

The art of befriending strangers

I believe everybody you meet comes into your life for a reason. Sometimes you just know you're going to be friends for life. Other times you realize it's just to make your experience in one place truly memorable. When you're traveling, you may meet a stranger who introduces you to someone you become very close with, or end up working with down the track.

When you look back on it and link up how you've come to know these people, it's often no coincidence. Or you meet people who provide you with a new perspective, challenge your way of thinking for the better or provide you with a lesson that stays with you forever.

In 2006 I met six guys on a long boat to Laos – the slowest 8-hour river ride ever. After drinking and playing cards and talking for the entire time we became a close-knit group of friends (with a gender ratio that was definitely in my favor).

We ended up traveling together for the majority of the next two weeks and it worked out perfectly. Each day, one of us would naturally assume group leader duties and come up with a fun plan of what we could do. Each of us had tales to tell from our adventures so far, and fortuitously we all got each others sense of humor and were on the same level of fun and smarts, which made it a joy to travel together.

Since then I've caught up with several of them back in their home countries and the memories will last a lifetime. In fact the whole reason I went biking across Africa in 2012 was due to a conversation with one of these guys on the slow boat, who told me all about it. Serendipity in action.

The best advice I can give you is to trust your gut when you meet people. Try not to judge strangers on first appearances or brief interactions as everyone reacts differently when they're away from home and traveling the world. Take an open and trusting stance with strangers. You'll have more rewarding relationships and friendships as a result. Plus it leads to all sorts of opportunities in life and business.

Talking about mixing business with pleasure, when you're based somewhere for a week or more don't forget to check the following sites to make new connections.

- **Couchsurfing.org** has a huge community of travelers and digital nomads that hold regular events in cities for members and non-members to join

- **Bizspora.com** as I outline in Chapter 13 is a great way to meet like-minded entrepreneurs around the world

- **Meetup.com** and **Eventbrite.com** are your go-to directories for global events and meet-ups happening around the world. You can search on location or category and then go and join in.

Co-working spaces are an excellent way to focus in on your work and meet fellow entrepreneurs, plus they're a great place to come up to speed with local events and get introductions.

> "I like to mix it up between co-working spaces and my apartment or cafes when I'm traveling or at home. I'm an introverted personality, so I sometimes find it hard to work with so many friends and peers around to distract me. The wonderful thing about co-working spaces and peer networks is that for someone like me, it is too easy to fall into the pattern of working alone. These places and communities force you to be around people who aren't offended when you stick headphones in your ears for 6 hours, as long as you occasionally pull them out to talk to the person across the table."
>
> *~ Elisa Doucette*

The realities of global relationships

But what if you're not a solo traveler and you have a partner to consider or a family? Well as an independent traveler, I'm no relationship expert, so I've covered all bases.

Solo travel

It is a lot easier when you're a solo traveler as you're likely to meet a lot more people if you're single. If you're part of the "Lonely Planet" brigade and following the same recommendations as thousands of others on what to see and do next, you'll easily find firm travel companions with which to share new experiences.

Of course leaving these new found friends behind can sometimes be tough to do. Even more so when you meet an amazing person while walking along the canals of Venice, on a star-filled evening, have an incredible time together, and then have to wave goodbye to them from a train early the next day, unlikely to cross paths again (sometimes that's a good thing too depending on how things went).

Challenges of being single include being hassled more in countries where it's common, like India and Morocco (especially for women), and if you get sick on the road there's no-one to help you out. Plus you can open yourself up to potential danger in countries where it's not safe to walk the streets on your own.

If you're traveling to remote parts of the world or you've set up a base for a long-term stay in a location that's off the beaten track you may get lonely from lack of personal interaction.

"There came a time when I was whimpering audibly when zipping my fattening suitcase. I knew it was time to rein it in when I was in Rome and felt, oh, sigh, another city. It was wonderful and it was lonely. It was enlightening and it was boring. The worst thing is that it looks so cool from the outside and inside it's just another facet of reality. I have no regrets; when I came home after a year as a nomad, I had more confidence than I'd ever have, and three years later, I still have it."

~ *Cynthia Morris*

Partners, married couples and friends

Nothing tests a relationship like traveling together. Spending 24 hours a day in each other's company is the quickest path to a lifetime of bliss or a nasty breakup. You learn everything there is to know about each other — both good and bad — and you see each other react to things in all sorts of different situations like stress, panic, joy and Full Moon beach parties.

Upsides include sharing the travel experience together, being there for each other and the sense of companionship you gain as you go on your own journeys together. If you're both online entrepreneurs then there's nobody better to understand your need to work while traveling.

Downsides are lack of time or space apart (depending on your travel plans) and fewer opportunities (unless you're particularly social) to meet as many people if you were solo and single.

The same applies to traveling with a friend, minus lovers' tiffs. You still learn a lot about each other and this can make or break a friendship. It's always a good idea, whether you're best buddies from childhood or new friends, to test traveling together on a short trip of a week or two, before you embark on an epic expedition of months or even years. You don't want your best friend turning into your latest nightmare.

Families

I'm a firm believer that if you've got kids, travel is always an option, as is relocating to another country to live and work. In fact, unless your toddler is a complete terror or has a medical condition that makes it impossible to travel, the younger you expose your children to travel, the better they will adapt to life on the road.

I'm not a parent, but I sure was a great kid and my parents took my sister and me on round-the-world trips when we were still in diapers. Just look at how well I turned out!

If you're not convinced, then check back in Chapter 3 on the Dennings, who are traveling the world with their five little munchkins. Ask your friends who travel with family what tricks they have up their sleeve to make it a rewarding experience. Your kids will be experientially richer when you open their eyes to the world.

So do you have a better and deeper understanding for what it means to travel the world and run your business from anywhere? Are you more excited than ever or rethinking your plans entirely?

Starting a business is such a personal thing, as is traveling the world. When the two mix it can be ecstasy or disaster, or something in between. It's really important for you to consider everything discussed in this chapter to ensure you know what to expect as a Suitcase Entrepreneur.

What on earth should you do now?

- Print off the pros and cons list, and answer those questions honestly

- Based on those results, consider your options for your location independent setup

- Depending on your level of experience in world travel, take time to talk with friends who have had similar experiences to those you're going to encounter

- Think hard about whether you're up for solo travel or with a partner

- Don't contact me for parental advice; I'm not your gal.

Chapter 11

Deciding on where to travel and your preparation checklist.

Tourists don't know where they've been,
travelers don't know where they're going.
~ PAUL THEROUX

There are so many factors to consider when setting off on your travels. The most important factor, though, is to know your travel and adventure preferences. Or let's call it your *nomadic quotient.*

Are you the type who enjoys fancy hotels or decadent resorts even if you can't really afford them? Or are you the type who likes to rough it on a tiny budget and hang with the locals?

As discussed in the last chapter, your unique travel style will depend upon many factors, including your tolerance for risk, your desired levels of comfort, your language preferences, your weather expectations and, of course, your budget.

In this chapter I'll attempt to:

- Break down the many facets of travel you need to consider

- Help you decide the best places to travel and to live

- Give you real-life examples to help you make the right choices.

Why travel cultivates happiness

Before we launch into all the finer details of where to travel to and what style of travel suits you, it's important to face the facts. It's a proven fact that travel does indeed cultivate happiness.

In 2013 G Adventures surveyed over two thousand people and found that 83% considered travel very important to their happiness. In fact 71% of all respondents felt that travel was more important to their happiness than retirement, having a baby, buying a car, getting married, being promoted or purchasing a home.

One thing's for sure: the more you travel, the better you get at it and the more instinctive it becomes. You become skilled at always being prepared, packing light, negotiating successfully and knowing the right transport options. You also become more adept at making decisions quickly.

"The good thing is, there are so many ways to be location independent and tweaking your approach can make massive improvements. My partner and I have now been on the road for nearly 7 years. Or actually, I should say — he has. He started off solo, and we met shortly thereafter, sharing a wanderlust that proved to be aligned. We travel in a RV, providing a home base that moves with us. We always have our own super comfy bed, know where the cups go and know where the extra toilet paper is stashed. We can choose our pace of travel, when we want to be introverted or around people, and switch up living in urban areas vs 'out in nature'. And when we want to travel away from home, we can park the house and fly off somewhere else for a bit."

~ *Cherie & Chris*

No matter where in the world you choose to go, my number one piece of advice is *to keep an open mind and always expect the unexpected.*

What style of travel suits you?

Do you want to work and travel, only travel, move around a lot, or stay put in one place for a month or two? Would you prefer to take extended trips throughout the year, do a home exchange, house-sit or relocate to a new place for an entire year or more?

Are you happy flying or do you prefer train travel or going green on a bicycle or travelling on foot? Do you get seasick or love being on the ocean? These are all good questions to ask yourself before you go leave home.

You'd be surprised at how many people take a cruise and spend the entire week throwing up overboard as they didn't know that they are prone to terrible seasickness, or who go to a tropical paradise only to find out that they are allergic to mosquito bites.

Are you a planner or a free spirit?

If you're into planning, knowing everything in advance and pre-booking your flights, accommodation and activities, then your travel experience will be completely different to the free spirit who just goes where the wind blows him.

I've done both and they each have their advantages and disadvantages. These days I've adopted the 'un-planning' style, where I choose to discover things as I go. That said, I'm naturally in a pre-packed state and have years of experience behind me that requires less planning overall.

I tend to book my flights in advance once I know where I'm going for the next 6 months. Largely I base my trips around countries I'm yet to visit, Ultimate Frisbee tournaments and other events. How about you?

> "There is still an assumption at large that traveling 'for pleasure' is a simple enough task. All one needs is a little spare time, money and one or two good addresses. Yet we're waking up to the idea that like most human activities, traveling is in fact an art which benefits from being systematically thought through and practiced.
>
> "We're getting better at learning how to structure journeys so that they can assuage what we're lacking within us. Pleasure is in the end as hard to reach as money is to earn. We owe it to ourselves to treat our travel ambitions with dignity – our journeys should be the midwives of new and better selves."
>
> ~ *Allain De Botton, author of The Art of Travel*

Where in the world do you want to travel?

This is so very personal to you. There are so many amazing countries to visit in the world that it can be hard to choose. Speaking from personal experience, all this choice can sometimes be your worst enemy. If only someone would say "You can only travel to this continent this year" it would make choosing where to go next a lot easier!

Ask yourself whether you're looking for tropical climes or cool mountain weather. This plays a really important role, not only in deciding where to go, but also in what activities to do and what to pack. Remember, no matter how many guidebooks or blogs you read on a place, nothing will ever replace experiencing it for yourself.

The *G Adventures* survey showed that the number one location in the world was Australasia (yeah that's right – Australia and my homeland New Zealand!). This was followed by Africa and Antarctica both coming in at #2, South America #3, Europe #4, Asia #5, North America, Central America and Middle East tied at #6.

Here's my quick and dirty guide on where to travel, based on my travel to 61 countries and my humble opinion:

- If you're looking for style, safety, comfort, cleanliness and great infrastructure, and you're not on a limited budget then head to northern European countries and Scandinavia.

- Southern European countries are great for being more relaxed, slightly cheaper and less structured than northern Europe, with great food, lots of history and excellent transport options.

- If you want a cheap place to live and travel, in comparison to the western world, but still friendly and relaxed, then head to South East Asia.

- If a generally cheap and challenging adventure is what you are after, then try the continent of Africa (that said, South Africa – especially Cape Town — is not particularly cheap).

- For a relatively cheap adventure that's great for backpacking, outdoor activities and a place where you can practice a new language as English is not as widely spoken, head to South America.

- To experience beautiful scenery, lots of outdoor activities, friendly people, and safe, easy travel options, but you are prepared to pay for it, then try New Zealand and Australia.

- If you want idyllic islands with varying levels of budget, safety and activities try the South Pacific, Thailand, Vietnam, Caribbean and the Mediterranean.

- North America is great for long distance road trips, the great outdoors, and all those other things you see in the movies like fast food, entertainment, all you can eat and all you can buy, plus business and conferences galore.

Still confused? Feast your eyes on TripAdvisor's Traveler's Choice of 2013 and in particular their *Top 25 Destinations to Visit in the World*. I've been to all but four of them — 15, 19, 21 and 22. What about you?

TripAdvisor profiles the best beaches, family vacations and hotels, so it's worthwhile taking a look to see what takes your fancy. While you're at it, check out TripAdvisor's forums and reviews from travelers on the places you're going to. I actually make my decisions on places I've never been to, based on other peoples' opinions.

What cultural experience are you looking for?

Do you want to experience a completely new culture or just take it easy and be in some place that's familiar? Are you traveling to a specific event or festival that you've heard about? Or are you intent on having a certain kind of lifestyle?

To me, the beauty of travel is exposing myself to new cultures and learning from them. It gives you a great perspective on your own life and helps you question what you take for granted or consider normal. It opens your eyes to how societies work and what underpins their value systems.

Unfortunately, I've seen too many travelers disrespect local cultures, customs and traditions, expecting things to be just as they are back at home, and getting frustrated when they're different. Be sure to choose your destinations wisely for your sake and for that of the locals. Why on earth would you go to China to eat McDonalds or expect that you can get the same things in supermarkets as you can back home?

How far does your budget stretch?

Are you happy to spend money by living it up in more expensive cities like New York, London, Amsterdam, Zurich, Sydney or Auckland? Or are you looking to travel on a shoestring, save money and live out of a backpack in cheaper destinations?

For example, it's easy to live like a king or queen for as little as US$10-20 a day in South East Asia, parts of central Asia, South America and throughout Africa. Here's an example from my travels:

> When I was in Thailand in 2013, I hired a Kawasaki Ninja 650cc motorbike to go from Chiang Mai to Chiang Rai for 3 days, at US$30 per day. However scooters cost a mere quarter of that price and use less gas. If you hire them for a period of a few weeks, you can get them as cheaply as US$2.50 per day.
>
> Massages are typically in the range of $3-5 for an entire hour. In the Philippines I had a full pedicure and manicure for the grand price of $2.50. I literally couldn't get over it! That was until I got a full week's gym membership in a less touristy part of Cebu for a total of $2.50.
>
> Later on, I visited the Shangri-La beach resort, which was 10-minute drive away. There, for a day pass to the hotel grounds and swimming pools including lunch, they were charging US$100 – totally catering to the well-off tourist.

In North America, even though some things are really cheap, your cost of living and travel will be closer to double that of the stories above.

In Europe your daily allowance is likely to be three to four times as much, even if you're traveling cheaply, as even hostels will cost you 15-20 Euros a night. It's good to know that you can generally negotiate great deals on longer-term stays though!

Naturally you can spend $1,000 on a fancy hotel or resort in many locations around the globe and pay hundreds of dollars for a top bottle of wine. It's totally up to you.

If you want to know how cheap or expensive a country is, you should visit McDonalds. It has become the barometer by which you can judge the value of your money (seriously , do this even if you hate McDonalds).

In France you'll pay around 7 Euros for a Big Mac Meal. (US$9.34 at today's exchange rate). In Malaysia this same combo will cost 9 Ringgit (US$3). Not only is McDonalds a great indicator for how much other fast food should cost you, but it's also a benchmark for prices in general.

Even the Economist has the *"Big Mac Index theory of purchasing-power parity"* which states that "in the long run, exchange rates should adjust to equal the price of a basket of goods and services in different countries".

Never judge a country by its Starbucks though. I mean this in all seriousness. No matter where in the world you go, Starbucks is always a rip off.

How key is communication?

How comfortable do you feel living in a country where you don't know the language? Is it part of your plan to learn a new language or do you want to be able to communicate freely and easily?

If you're a native English speaker then this makes things a lot easier, as most people defer to English as the global language of choice. But there are still many places in the world where hand signals, body language and facial expressions are the only way to communicate, and, indeed, that may be just what you're looking for.

Do you depend on certain services and amenities?

Depending upon your business and lifestyle, do you want a firmly established infrastructure in place where Internet is in abundance (for example, in Hong Kong)?

Do you want to access co-working spaces and all the facilities that come with them and work amongst a startup crowd? Or are you ok with just a laptop, a wireless dongle and Internet connection that comes and goes like ocean waves lapping at your feet?

If medical services are important to you then you will definitely need to consider carefully the locations you choose to travel to or base yourself. The cost of medical expenses in some countries can be incredibly reasonable, like my doctor's visit and prescription in Kuala Lumpur for less than US$15. But on the other hand, medical expenses can be through the roof in other places.

How important is your food?

Do you have specific requirements when it comes to the types of food you eat, or are you a food lover, on a mission to taste anything and everything?

Whenever I dine with other people on the road, I'm surprised at how difficult finding suitable meals can be for vegetarians, especially in South America where meat is in plentiful supply, and also in some Asian countries where your options are meat with rice or noodles.

Gluten-free vegans will love the food in Vietnam; seafood fans will enjoy Japan and many countries in South East Asia, as well as the island nations around the world like the South Pacific. In Africa you often get what's given to you in the smaller towns and once again, vegetarian options aren't always plentiful.

I shot a fun video on YouTube on how to find the best food when travelling abroad to help you out.

My first round the world trip

One of my favorite things in the world is listening to other peoples' travel stories. You often learn a lot about a destination you haven't yet visited, as well as about the person you're speaking to. If you asked four people who had all been on exactly the same trip, they would tell completely different stories about their experiences.

So let me tell you a story.

In 2003 I set out on a solo round-the-world trip armed with a large backpack, a sense of adventure, and a little trepidation. While I'd already done a lot of traveling before, this was a 4-month trip to Europe, North America, Russia and South America, and it was going to be the longest time I'd been away from home by myself.

I'd bought a round-the-world ticket that included 24 connecting flights across these continents from my local travel agent for around NZ $2,500. All the flight legs were open-ended and could be changed along the way, but I had departure and arrival dates into each city.

The Lonely Planet was my bible. I had bought one for Europe and one for South America, and had read them religiously in advance of my trip, every night or morning. I had planned my activities around the recommendations in the books, and wanted to do everything suggested.

As a result of relying on Lonely Planet, I met a host of other backpackers and travelers doing exactly the same things as I was doing and who then suggested other activities. My travel became somewhat of an adventure, based upon other people's experiences and recommendations.

Along the way I met up with people traveling a similar route to mine, and so we buddied-up on sharing rooms and transport, and spent time swapping travel stories.

The key lessons learned

The good:

Some of the joys of traveling are the random experiences you'll have, either by yourself or with others. Many of the people I met became good friends and I've since been to visit them in their hometowns or I have happened to meet up with them again, somewhere around the world years later. Others I'll likely never see again.

This is what I love most about travel: the unexpected bonuses that you could never anticipate; the experiences you would not have had otherwise; the interesting people you were not specifically planning on meeting.

Traveling as a single female has been a great way to meet people, especially couples who have 'adopted' me on the next leg of their journey. It's often easier to meet people when traveling alone, When you're part of a duo or small group, fewer people approach you since you're already engaged in conversation or already have firm plans.

I have been very lucky in that I have never felt unsafe in places where I was warned to take particular care, for example in Rio de Janeiro, Brazil, where I was told not to take the public transport and not to walk the streets alone at night (I did both). Nor did I feel at all at risk in Ecuador, Peru, Bolivia, Argentina or Chile, but I did make sure to keep my wits about me and keep my valuables out of site.

In fact I have always felt as safe as if I were in my home town of Wellington (I'm pretty tall and athletic for a woman) aside from one taxi ride from the Mexico City airport to the hostel, where I witnessed my first aftermath of a shooting.

The not so good:

I actually ended up cutting this round-the-world trip short. Originally I had intended it to be a six-month trip, but by the time I got to Chile I was nearly out of money and was frankly tired of packing up my backpack every single day and being constantly on the move. I'd covered such a distance and was exhausted.

With hindsight, I should have started with the South American leg, whilst I had the energy and should have finished off in Europe. South America is an amazing continent and a natural adventure playground, so it requires a lot of energy and an adventurous attitude.

Travel by bus is readily available but some roads are dangerous and pot-holed. Flights are expensive and long, and boat trips are fun but slow.

Compare that to Europe where traveling by train, plane, bus or rental car is beyond easy, efficient and affordable. While I was there I had set myself up with a cushy month of traveling.

The flipside was that I had also spent my money a lot faster than I had planned to do in Europe, due in part to having stayed in Hostelerias' (one up from a hostel and one down from a hotel) for around 25-50 Euros a night.

The fact that every Euro spent was almost NZ$3 meant that my money disappeared really quickly. In fact, from memory, the entire trip cost around NZ $10,000 over those four months, which compared to what I would have paid in living costs back home anyway.

The pro traveler's trip, 10 years on

Ten years later, from January to April 2013, I spent time in Malaysia, Thailand, Brunei, the Philippines and South Korea and I never consulted one guidebook even once. So long as my travels took me to places I hadn't been to before and allowed me to play in several Ultimate Frisbee tournaments, I was happy.

On this trip I often just went with the flow, taking recommendations from friends or simply asking my social media buddies for suggestions, which was the reason why I found myself flying 12 hours from Amsterdam to Kuala Lumpur, Malaysia on New Year's Day in the first place!

Based on a TripAdvisor recommendation I stayed at a great guesthouse called Sarang Vacay Homes. Soon after arriving I was met by two local tour guides, Seh Hui and Yongjue. I had not met either of them in person before but I had come to know them through my blog and also a personal introduction (thanks Pam Slim!). One was a featured change maker in my $100 Change program, and the other had bought and participated in this same program. How cool is that?

They took me on a local tour of their city and then proceeded to put me in contact with friends of theirs wherever I went next. So while visiting Penang for a 7 day digital sabbatical, I had a personal guide named Khoo who showed me the National Park and the historical George Town.

Khoo then introduced me to Ai Ching, the founder of Piktochart (a very cool infographic tool I use) and her whole team. I had no idea they were even based in that area!

Adventures from un-planning

This next amusing story highlights just how differently I travel a decade after my first world trip. While in Kuala Lumpur, I asked my lovely hosts at the guesthouse for a suggestion on where I could go to concentrate on writing this very book, since they had already been so helpful with other advice and had also been storing my bag for me when I headed off, taking only a small backpack.

They suggested an organic farm hideaway called The Kebun. It looked beautiful on the website and the price of US$20 a night included all meals, a room in a longhouse and the use of a car!

I was sold. There were so many things to do around that Sarawak area like seeing orangutans, turtles, monkeys and the world's largest flower, the Rafflesia, as well as numerous national parks to hike in.

My hosts told me that I just needed to fly to Kuching, so I booked it online via Air Asia's website (the budget airline equivalent to EasyJet for Asia) and headed off a few days later. It was only while on the flight that I looked at the map in the inflight magazine and realized that I was actually headed to Borneo Island, Malaysia.

I hadn't even thought to check where I might be going on a map, just assuming that my destination was south of Kuala Lumpur. I have never been so uninformed about where I was going to in my life; quite ironic for a "renowned world traveler".

Yet it worked out perfectly. It sparked a new desire in me to select the *Everywhere option'* the next time I book through Skyscanner.net, allowing random chance to pick a destination for me to head off to, of which I have no knowledge.

Top tip: I think this is a style of travel that could catch on. Sometimes the best adventures in life come from not knowing what will happen next. If you'd like some help with this, check out my friends who invented the Zufall dice – you simply roll two dice to help you make your next decision on where you may head, and leave it to chance.

While I was on Borneo Island, part of both Malaysia and Indonesia, I realized that I could easily make my way to Brunei, a small country also on the island. From there I could head further north to Kota Kinabalu and play in an Ultimate Frisbee tournament that just happened to be on a few weeks later.

From Borneo Island it's not that far to the Philippines, another country I had not yet visited. Some clients of mine who live there suggested that CebuAir was a good and affordable airline to fly with and so I found myself in Manila.

I was excited to arrive in Manila and to finally meet up with a bunch of people I'd brought together for the occasion: Clement had designed my website back in 2011; Prime had bought several of my programs; Janet had designed eBooks for me, had taken my $100 Change program and had won a $500 business scholarship through that program; and Rick, who I didn't know, but who was on my latest Frisbee team.

The very next day I was on another flight, this time to Boracay Island, where I was signed up to play at one of the best Beach Ultimate Tournaments in South East Asia.

All this had happened by putting the word out, looking into tournaments, and being accepted on a team. I had also been invited to play on a team in another tournament, this time in Jeju, South Korea.

I hadn't yet visited South Korea but a great friend from my London days was living in Busan, so I headed there from the Philippines. I stayed with my friend for close to two weeks, and played in another fantastic competitive tournament where we even made the finals!

My un-planning and allowing things to come together gave me some of my best experiences and memories to date. It also helps to have a network of friends on social media and contacts through your own various interest groups and activities.

The main trick is to *ask*. People are all too happy to give you information. I ask my friends for recommendations, and ask the locals also. You never know what will come out of it; being put up for a night or two with a friend of a friend, offers to attend events or festivals or even house-sitting opportunities.

> "Travel is like crack. Three years ago I would have never dreamt that I would have seen the places I've seen. But now that I have and I know how easy it is to travel, I want it all. "Northern Lights? I wanna see 'em. "Machu Pichu? Sign me up. "Thailand? Let's do it. "With technology and a little know how, the world truly is our playground. But where do we stop? Do we ever stop? And how much is enough?"
>
> ~ *Mike Hrostoski*

What you need to know before you go

Now that you have a better idea of where you want to head to, it's a good idea to get a few things in order and prepare the basics. Here's a list of things to consider and research before you go:

• Visa requirements

• Vaccinations

- Political stability –

- Weather & Climate

- Language(s) spoken and religion

- Electricity supply

- Internet connectivity — speed, stability, availability & cost

- Currency and ATM availability

- Basic costs of living (food, transport and accommodation).

I have to recommend Google for getting quick and useful answers, and Lonely Planet's online resources (plus their in-depth country and city guides) for fantastic information on all of these areas.

What essentials you need

To make it easier on yourself, here are the key things you need to think about before you pack up and head off on your journey. I've put all this, and more, into a handy pre-flight checklist which you can download from my website.

Essentials checklist:

- Passport and Visas

- Vaccinations, medications

- Health and/or travel insurance

- Local currency, extra cash and credit card(s)

- Copies of all important documents (online and paper)

- Notice given to your bank of your travel destinations

- Itinerary and contact details available to friends or family.

Let's go into these things in more depth and break it down so we're on the same page. In Chapter 13 I elaborate on what to actually pack.

Passports

This is the one thing you simply can't leave home without. Along with money, this is all you really need to travel. Everything else can be bought en-route. Here are my top passport tips:

- Check your passport is not due to expire within six months. If it is then you need to get a new one. Some countries are real sticklers for this, and even though the passport is technically valid, they won't permit you to travel.

- Allow yourself up to a month to get a new passport (depending on where you live). If you need a quick turnaround you can pay for an express service of 1-3 days.

- Check the number of blank pages you have left. Some countries are a pedantic about this and will refuse you entry if you don't meet their empty-page criterion.

- Treat your passport well and put it in a pouch or travel wallet. Custom officials do not like passports that are rough around the edges or have any peeling pages. This can indicate tampering and they may even deny you entry or take your passport from you – I know from personal experience.

Visas

Whether you require a visa to visit a country depends upon your nationality and their visa terms. The best and simplest thing to do is to Google that country's government site or a key resource website, telling you which countries require your nationality to have a visa. A useful site to check is visahq.com to apply for visas.

I'm fortunate to have two of the best passports to travel on in terms of international relations and free visas; New Zealand (no enemies anywhere) and United Kingdom (hello to working in almost all of Europe). These passports have helped me out on several occasions.

Remember my first world trip in 2003? Well here's a story to highlight the importance of having the right visa when you're traveling.

To Russia with love illegally

I spent 5 amazing days in Russia in 2003, during the "white nights" when daylight almost never ends, and I had a delightful time exploring Moscow and St Petersburg with my good friend.

On the way to the airport, I decided to check my flight itinerary one more time and realized that my flight was in fact on the following day. I started laughing but then quickly became aware that my visa actually ran out on that current day.

Let's face it, I'd seen all the villains in those Bond movies, so the last country in the world I wanted to be stuck in illegally was Russia, even though my interactions with the locals had been warm and friendly.

What's more, this particular visa had been a pain in the ass to get hold of. I'd had to visit the Russian Embassy in New Zealand, pay a large amount of money and then wait. They had taken so long to issue the visa, over three weeks in fact, that I had had to leave New Zealand on my UK passport and have Dad send my NZ passport, complete with visa, to catch up with me in Europe.

My friend told me not to worry, and that they'd want me out of the country as much as I now wanted to leave. So we went to a hostel, and as I checked in at the booth the lady hissed at me with a dramatic one-liner, the likes of which you imagine hearing only in the movies;

"No, you cannot stay. You must leave Russia by midnight!" And with that she promptly slammed the window shut. I stood there in shock. Once I had snapped out of it, and upon talking to a travel agent at a desk in the lobby, I realized that it was impossible to leave.

To avoid any such situation, I suggest you double-check the visa requirements before you leave your current location, and definitely before you're due to arrive.

When you're traveling it's often more difficult to be able to get to an embassy or to sort out a visa over the phone. But luckily, depending upon your passport, many countries just offer a visa to you on entry, at no extra charge.

Most visas last for at least 2 weeks and more commonly for 30 days or three months. If you overstay your visa you can usually extend it in the country you're in for a fee, or get hit up with a hefty fee at the airport. Money can buy you out of many situations and it's unlikely you'll be thrown in jail, like many people seem to think. But you don't ever want to put yourself in that situation in the first place.

An example of extending my visa happened during my trip to the Philippines, where they issue everyone with a standard 21-day visa upon entry into the country at no charge. I had actually forgotten to check this before arriving and then realized that I'd be overstaying by 6 days.

Had I done my research, I would have booked to leave on an earlier flight. It turned out that I could extend my visa for over 30 days, costing around US$70 and being processed within a day.

Travel tickets

It is important to know that, as a condition of entry, many countries require you to show proof of onward travel in the form of a ticket, be it flight, bus, train or boat.

I appreciate sometimes you may not know where you're going next, but whatever, you need to have a plan of action or a really good story to convince immigration!

Insurance

For many years I traveled around with no insurance (I'm sure all North Americans reading this will be gasping in shock). I put this down to growing up with a father who was a top insurance salesman in his day and never insured our family against anything.

Unless you have really valuable items with you, like jewelry and/or expensive electronic equipment, it's highly unlikely that the cost of losing one or two items, or even your whole suitcase full of clothes, is going to end your life.

That said, if you're going off to more dangerous parts of the world, or those with expensive hospital bills, it pays to have some form of travel insurance that also includes medical cover.

If you're going somewhere with a lack of infrastructure or facilities, then consider a policy that incudes emergency evacuation and repatriation.

After much research, I personally recommend World Nomads. They repeatedly come out on top for the best medical and personal cover. I paid US$600 for a one-year world-wide travel insurance policy, including adventure activities (like cycling across Africa) and additional cover for my laptop and smartphone.

Check with your credit card company too, especially if you're on a reward program. They often have a travel insurance plan or program that is either free or for which you can pay a little extra.

I, for one, wouldn't want to have an accident in the United States and end up with a medical bill of at least US$10,000. But in other countries visiting the doctor or having surgery can be a massive cost saving compared to where you normally live. Why do you think people head to other countries for major dental work, laser eye surgery and cosmetic enhancements?

Currency and cards

From a travel perspective, it's good to have more than one credit card with you, and that goes for debit cards too. It pays to keep them in different places in case your wallet or bag gets stolen, so that you don't lose them all at once.

There's nothing more frustrating than your bank putting your card on hold due to suspicious activity when you're traveling. This is usually triggered by making multiple transactions in a foreign country or multiple withdrawals from ATMs within a short space of time.

Every time you travel, and every few months, it is a good idea to ring your bank and give them your itinerary for them to make a special note of it in their system. However, even with this protection in place it can still happen that they stop your card without notice, or worse yet, cancel it

When I was writing this book in Lapu Lapu, the Philippines, I received an email saying that my US debit card had not only been stopped but had been canceled due to suspicious activity. They told me that they were sending a replacement, which wasn't helpful given the address they were using was a friend's the US, where I wouldn't be until months later.

At the time that card had been my main source of accessing cash, as few places accepted credit cards. My New Zealand bank account, which I rarely use, had zero funds but my UK one, which I hadn't been using for quite a while had just enough to get me through the weekend until I could talk to my US bank. If I hadn't have had these options I literally would have been screwed.

Backup copies

I highly recommend carrying photocopies of your passport, insurance policy and driver's license. You should have these in print format and I recommend using Dropbox for electronic versions. I share this folder with my family and one key friend whom I can trust, which is useful, especially if I'm going somewhere more dangerous.

It also pays to keep copies of receipts for big ticket items like your laptop, smartphone, tablet or digital camera, otherwise you could be hit up for a duty fee, especially if you can't prove that they weren't purchased in the country you're visiting. I've never had this happen as such, but nor would I want to be in that situation. Once again share these receipts on Dropbox, Evernote, Shoeboxed or whichever electronic medium you choose, but preferably one that synchronises with the cloud and your devices.

If you're fairly new to travel you should refer to this chapter often and heed the lessons I've learned the hard way, so that you don't have to experience them for yourself.

Essential actions to take now

- Download the Essentials Checklist from **suitcaseentrepreneur.com/book/resources** Chapter 11 and save it in your 'Travel folder' in the cloud so that you can access it at anytime.

- Consider your next trip preparation and whether you need to update your passport or apply for a visa now.

- Look into travel insurance options through World Nomad or a local company catering to your nationality.

- Do your research and indulge in travel guides and online resources as well as forums, to get a real idea of your planned or potentially un-planned itinerary.

Chapter 12

The art of minimalism and how to pack for anywhere.

Travel, I was coming to realize, was a metaphor not only for the countless options life offers but also for the fact that choosing one option reduces you to the parameters of that choice. Thus, in knowing my possibilities, I also knew my limitations.

~ ROLF POTTS

One thing that always makes me smile, laugh, or stare incredulously, is how other people pack for their travels. At airports I am often amazed at how much crap people drag with them.

When I see one couple taking four massive suitcases with them, I seriously wonder if they also packed their kitchen sink. There's a tendency towards excess in this world, and that applies to packing too.

You rarely need as much as you think you do. In fact, the less you take, the more you'll enjoy your travels. The next time you're at an airport or train station and you see a business or leisure traveler with just one small bag, take note: this person practices the art of minimalism and so should you. Once you start, it's incredibly freeing.

In this chapter you'll learn

- The art of minimalism and what this really means for you

- How to pack for any trip like a pro

- All you need to prepare before you reach your destination.

The importance of minimalism

When people ask me why I live out of just one suitcase, I tell them it makes me feel free. There's nothing more liberating than being able to pack your entire life up in 20 minutes and know you can move on at a moment's notice.

When I stay with friends and family who've been firmly entrenched in their homes for several years, I look at all their possessions and think "Man, how long would this take to pack up?"

Then I ask myself "What does all this stuff mean to them? Is it kept for nostalgic reasons? Does it define who they are? Is it to show others what they wish to represent to the world?"

Despite what you may think, I do actually understand that some creature comforts enrich your life. I understand that it's lovely to have a base where you are surrounded by things you hold dear and that make you feel at home, and accepted.

But I'm talking about the extra junk that you've just accumulated for the sake of it. That stuff actually stresses me out. There have been studies conducted that prove that having a clean, uncluttered and simple space to live and work in, makes you more productive and happy.

> "Minimalist living is counter-cultural. It is contrary to every advertisement we have ever seen because we live in a society that prides itself on the accumulation of possessions. But there is far more joy to be found in the pursuit of fewer possessions than can ever be discovered in the pursuit of more."
>
> ~ Joshua Becker, **Becoming Minimalist**

Benefits of minimalism

- You spend less money, as you simply don't need to accumulate extras, just the essentials. You actually have more financial freedom

- You're less stressed as you don't have to look after, or feel weighed down by all the things you own

- You feel more freedom as a result of having fewer things.

- You save time by not having to clean up or maintain so many things and as a result you become more productive

- It's good for the environment since the less you consume, the less damage is done to the environment (and hopefully less waste is produced).

Your essential packing list

Packing is truly an art. Much like travel, the more you do of it, the better you should become. Once you've experienced lugging a giant suitcase behind you on a sandy path to your island resort, or have stood in line at airport security watching a customs officer unpack every single item that took you three hours to meticulously squeeze into your bag in the first place, you'll appreciate this skill.

If you're a sun worshipper then it's going to be much easier to pack light and take less with you. Generally countries with warmer weather tend to be more relaxed cultures, so there is less need to dress up. You can get away with swimwear, a sarong, flip flops and a variety of outfits made out of light materials that weigh next to nothing and take up little room.

If you're heading off hiking, mountain climbing or skiing then you have a whole set of new considerations around which you'll need to pack, organize and prepare for. Of course your bag will be bulkier and your gear will be heavier.

If your travels entail part business, part leisure, you can definitely 'cross-dress', so to speak, and mix and match items. I've never been one for adhering to 'suiting up' like everyone else in order to present a professional front. You can take one smart jacket, a pair of pants or skirt and that should do the trick.

Understanding the environment you'll be travelling to will make all the difference to what you pack

Getting started packing:

Once you've laid out what you want to take, get ruthless and take out any extra' items you've put in that you think you might need. Usually this is the 5th dress, the 7th t-shirt, or the extra pair of shoes or shorts.

If you're no good at this, bring in the heavies. Ask your friends, family, your partner, or someone else who will say "no", even when you put up a fight: "Do you really think I'm going to need or wear this?"

You will find that, unless you're Paris Hilton, you'll end up wearing your same favorite outfits over and over again. So:

• Take one outfit that you can wear in a casual situation, one for business attire, one that makes you feel pretty, sexy or handsome and one that's comfy for travelling in.

- Make sure that you can throw all these items together in the washing machine without any drama.

- Choose fabrics that don't need to be ironed and that you can roll up in your suitcase or backpack that will stay relatively crease free.

- Linen and rayon are not your travel friends. Wool (and knit fabrics in general) and synthetics work great.

- Take travel size containers to put your skincare, creams and gels in (or buy travel size kits at the airport or pharmacy). This reduces weight and space dramatically.

> **Top tip:** I'm a huge fan of Icebreaker, which produces casual- and sports-wear including undergarments. Made with New Zealand Merino wool, their clothes are highly durable and never smell, even after months of sweating in them but not washing them – seriously, they've done tests! Icebreaker gear keeps you warm in winter and cool in summer and you can layer it up.

Now pack your suitcase, bag or backpack. Do you have room to buy stuff and fit more things in while traveling or is it crammed to the brim already? If you have no space and it's really heavy then I advise you to take it all out and eliminate more items.

Trust me, you rarely wear everything you take with you and if you do need anything else, you can almost always buy it in the destination you're going to.

The few exceptions here are:

- Quality shoes – if you have a very small or large foot

- Sunscreen — oddly this is one item that can be really expensive even in poorer countries, and the types of spectrum and quality are often limited

- Medical supplies – you want to bring your medicines with you in case you can't get a prescription, as well as contact lens solutions and a basic first aid kit never goes amiss. I recommend The Travel Doctor

- Electronic supplies – like cords and cables for your specialist equipment if it can't be easily replaced

- Take a dry bag, useful for putting in the electronics or other valuables, and doubling as a small day bag on trips when you don't want your items to get wet.

Here's what Dan Andrews has to say about dry bags:

> "I'm always around the water so it's got a lot of obvious benefits for beach trips and boating. It's fantastic for dirty and wet items you want to put in your pack. It can also work as a separator in your pack for your dirty shoes (if you've got them). These things are cheap, don't take up any space, and are *super* useful.

If you're looking for a more practical version of the little black bag check out these handy packing tips from Kristi Hemmer:

"After living three years around the world out of one duffel bag, I am a packing expert. If you need it, I have it.

"Let's start with the North Face BaseCamp Duffle Bag. It is waterproof, chicken bus worthy, can be locked, doesn't have exterior pockets to tempt thieves or you to overstuff, and has backpack straps for easy mobility. I can run for the bus no problem with this bag. Try doing that with wheels!

"I love packing cubes. I used to pack "instant outfits" into Ziploc bags but the plastic is noisy and created roomie problems. Packing cubes are vented, zip, and are like dresser drawers. I carry four: one for workout clothes, one for undergarments, one for 'going out' clothes, and one the rest.

Get your essential packing list

If I can live out of my suitcase for over 3 years full-time, and keep downsizing, you can go on holiday with less than 20kg.

All you really need is:

- Passport and money

- Clean underwear

- Basic toiletries

- Layers of light but warm clothing

- One 'decent' outfit that passes for going out at night

- One outfit that passes for business attire

- One decent pair of shoes, flip flops and exercise shoes

- Essential electronics

The rest is an added extra.

Just for you though, I've put together a full packing list you can download in the resources section of my book site under Chapter 11.

This is a complete checklist of items to remember to bring which are essential. I've made sure to include toiletries, shoes, electronics and added extras that you may need depending on your destination like an umbrella, poncho, money belt or mosquito net.

Once again, I do like Kristi's suggested items and her novel uses for each one of them (also included in the packing checklist you can download):

Here are some other key items:

Duct tape –this is a must have (my friend used it to close a deep wound when no doctor was available in Vanuatu)

Floss (a clothesline, measuring tape for buying clothes), *nail clippers* (cuts like scissors)

Wet wipes (for all the disgusting things you get yourself into), *sarong* (acts as a sheet, towel-dries fast, great for temples when you need to cover up)

Closed toe shoes (Try Keens which are sandals, shoes, waterproof, comfortable, and good looking)

Coat (for cold buses, pillow, and rain-I have a puffer one that folds into its pocket)

Fake wedding ring (saves me a lot of grief traveling)

Arriving at your destination

Without wanting to turn into a full-blown travel book, there are a number of things you can do before you arrive at your destination that will make your life much easier.

Remember that you might not have access to the Internet or a phone for some time, so don't rely on things you can only access when you're connected.

At the airport

When you first arrive at immigration you'll need to have the address of where you're staying to hand, and often a printed itinerary or receipt of onwards travel. If you don't have proof, at least have a back up story in place, like the fact that you'll be catching an overnight bus from the border on a certain date.

Get local currency

It's handy to have some spare change in the local currency before you arrive. You may not be able to access a foreign exchange or a working ATM quickly and then you'll be stranded. Trust me, I've seen plenty of people in this situation and have even had this issue myself once or twice.

I now keep a small money pouch that has around 30 different currencies in it. I regularly check through it before I fly somewhere, to see if I have a few spare notes to use just in case. The back-up plan is to access cash at the airport before you exit the terminal, either from an ATM or a foreign exchange, but don't count on this.

Get smart connections

Before you take off in a plane or cross over a border, turn off roaming on your mobile phone to avoid hefty costs. Don't forget to stop your local hot-spot or geo-location services, which can suck credit and data from a local SIM without you knowing.

If you have a smartphone, it's a great idea to have it unlocked since then you can simply buy a local SIM card and add credit for calls and texts, or data. I still think this is the most simple and cost-effective option when traveling. I usually do this at the airport.

Currently I have 10 different SIM cards which I keep in a small business card case, so that when I return to a country I can just reinsert the SIM. I usually ask a local for the best company to deal with or ask friends online. In general they're cheap to buy and load up.

You can also buy a mobile that has dual SIMs, so you can always keep your main SIM from home in, and add the local SIM too. If this all sounds like too much hassle try these international SIM cards:

- **OneSimCard** *is an International SIM card* with free incoming calls in 150 countries and outgoing calls priced from $0.25/min and data from $0.20/MB

- **GoSim** *has international SIM cards from $19, with cheap calls from 29c per min and data from 49c per MB, and with coverage in 185 countries.*

- **WorldSIM** allows you to make and receive *international* calls on your mobile without incurring expensive charges. You can check on their website for ideas of rates, depending on where you're calling from and to.

Taking public transport

At most airports, train stations and ferry terminals you can find taxis, shuttle buses, public buses, trains or underground options. As you'd expect, public transport is usually substantially cheaper but takes a lot longer. This is the one thing I do recommend you research in advance and usually the airport website is the best source of information.

In some countries, especially South East Asia, taxis are so cheap that it's just easier to take one than mess with public transport. In Europe and North America there is usually an abundance of transport options, so it makes sense to take the train or bus.

At Manila airport I headed straight to the information desk, asked for the approximate cost of a taxi to my hotel and found out it was $300-400 PHP (US$8-10).

Then I headed outside to the "official" taxi rank. I showed the friendly concierge the Google map coordinates of my hotel from my iPhone.

He quoted four times as much as the lady had. I was glad I had checked with her first. Turning back to the security lady I asked, *"Where are the legitimate non tourist taxis?"* This type of direct question doesn't always get you somewhere, but on this occasion she was good enough to let me know that I would find local taxis at the departure level. I did have to wait 30 minutes in a long queue, but the journey only took 15 minutes, not the quoted 45-60 minutes, and it was dead cheap.

Top Tip: Always have music, a Kindle book on your smartphone or Kindle device, a real book, or a podcast like mine to read/listen to when you know you will experience waiting times. It saves your sanity and makes you more productive.

Have emergency numbers handy

It's always good to have a friend's contact details in your phone saved as an emergency contact. You may also want to add in the local taxi company number, your local embassy number and the emergency hotline for police, ambulance, or fire.

If you want to make sure you can always make calls, then check out **SpareOne,** the only mobile phone that you can use anywhere in the world, with a lifespan of 15 years, that just requires one AA battery. It also has a built-in-flashlight and a dedicated emergency services dial button. You just put a in local SIM and you're off.

Sort accommodation

For general peace of mind it's a good idea to have at least your first night's accommodation booked. I remember on my 2003 world trip, after 54 hours of transit time, I arrived in Madrid at 11pm with nowhere to stay. A kind couple I'd met at the airport told me I could accompany them to their accommodation and see if there was a room.

Sadly there wasn't, and I ended up roaming the streets, with a large back-pack, late at night, knocking on doors and testing out my basic Spanish skills. It was not a great experience, especially when I was that tired, jet-lagged and all alone.

Now I always book ahead using TripAdvisor for recommendations and Agoda.com or Booking.com for good deals.

Always have the address to hand, the phone number, clear directions there or even better, a map. Don't assume taxi drivers know where they're going.

Use Google Maps:

Either before you go or once you're there, use the handy 'search nearby' function on Google maps to find a supermarket, café, WI-FI hotspot, pharmacy, police station, post office, or whatever service is important to you.

Download the app for your smartphone and search on where you want to go from your current location. What's even cooler is that on your iPhone you can still use this, even if you don't have Internet. The GPS location will still work so you can track the blue dot, in relation to the map, so long as you mistakenly lose the map off your phone.

Better yet, take a snapshot of this map on your mobile as a back up (on an iPhone hold down the button on top and the round front screen button at the same time). This has helped me out on numerous occasions.

Top tip: Mission abort plan

"Your mission abort plan' is something you hope you'll never need but it's crucial to have in place nonetheless…we used ours a couple of times, and were greatly relieved to have at least thought one through *before* we needed it!

"Your mission abort plan needs to cover what you might do, should everything go wrong and you need to head somewhere "safe". You need to consider:

• A preferred "emergency" destination

• The plane fare to your emergency destination

• Three months of expenses

• Emergency contact & accommodation."

~ Lea Woodward, locationindependent.com

Learn the basics of the local language

Since I'm often only in one country for a few days or weeks, I have to admit that I have become a little lazy with learning new languages, relying on my decent German and basic Spanish as much as I can.

It does go a long way though, to be able to say the basics in the local language and it can actually add a whole new dimension to your understanding and enjoyment of a local culture.

Naturally 'hello', 'goodbye', 'please' and 'thank you', are a great start. It's also good to try short phrases like 'How do I get to', or 'Where is the toilet/station/restaurant?'

Be prepared to receive an answer back in the local language, which is where it usually gets tricky. It's one thing attempting to speak a language, but entirely another to understand it. When in doubt, lots of hand gesturing and miming comes in handy, and repeating your question in a variety of different ways, using different words.

Even if you think you're not a natural at languages, you can make learning a language a whole lot more fun if you follow language hacker Benny Lewis's tips:

Language Hacking Tips

"*Before* going to the country get a head start with your language. Not just by doing a course, but by genuine contact with people. I can highly recommend the website italki.com to get either free language exchanges or very affordable private lessons over Skype.

"Start speaking from the day you decide to learn the language (no "I'm not ready" excuses!), and you will hit the ground running when you *do* arrive! While you are trying to speak do not be afraid to make mistakes! In real world use it's quite fine to conjugate your verb wrong, or use the wrong word.

"Native speakers in most countries are *incredibly* friendly and patient and will try to understand what you mean despite mistakes. Don't try to make it about speaking as correctly as possible, but about *getting your point across.*

"And keep in mind that everything you do study-wise (between spoken sessions) should be geared towards improving your immediate spoken skills, not for some distant point in the future.

"Leave complex grammar rules aside because grammar just helps us speak *correctly*, but vocabulary and set phrases are the "meat" of how we can truly communicate. Generally, I would recommend just getting a Lonely Planet phrasebook (or their phrasebook app) and studying that between spoken sessions."

~ Benny Lewis, Fluent in 3 Months

Better yet, I highly recommend you grab a copy of Benny's Language Hacking Guide.

So do you feel prepared and are you packed for freedom?

From minimalism to the art of packing, to landing and feeling like you are prepared for anything, this chapter has covered a lot. Naturally this was geared towards you if you've done less traveling and were looking for tips, or are branching out into more adventurous journeys.

If you were seeking something more strategic or advanced then you are making travel more complex then it needs to be. It all comes down to personal experiences and figuring out what's best for you, your style of travel, your choice of destinations and your levels of comfort with having less. And remember, when it comes to packing, less is more.

Packing it all together

- Download and print the Complete Packing Checklist (or save to your cloud syncing device of choice in electronic format)

- Go out and buy your travel size containers and the supplies that you need for your destination of choice – in advance

- When you're packing for your next trip, take a look around at what you've accumulated and pack an extra bag that you can take to a second-hand store or giveaway to a thrift or charity shop

- Refer back to Chapter 11 for your essentials preparation list and tips, and take a look at Chapter 13 for key travel tools I recommend for every aspect of your journey.

Chapter 13

Travel hacking tips and tools to save you time and money.

Travel is the only thing you buy that makes you richer.
~ ANONYMOUS

I posted the above quote on my Facebook page once. It got a lot of likes and shares, but also caused a heated discussion. Travel may not be the "only" thing that makes you richer, but I would argue that it's one of the best educations money can buy.

As we saw in the last chapter, travel does not have to be expensive. In fact if you travel to some of the parts of the world outlined in Chapter 11 like South East Asia, it's going to be cheaper to rent, to get around or to buy groceries than in your hometown.

What's more, travel will only continue to get cheaper as new forms of cost-effective transport emerge and competition heats up to offer tourists and hardcore travelers the best deals possible.

So let's get into the nitty gritty about spending as little as possible on your new travel adventures.

In this chapter you'll learn:

• Travel hacking tips from the professionals

• Top tools and services for accommodation and travel deals

• The best way to deal with Internet and Wi-Fi on the go

• Protecting your assets and valuables on your travels

• Travel accessories you won't want to leave home without.

Travel hacking tips

Would you believe me if I told you that there are people in this world who constantly travel for next to nothing? They're travel hackers; the geeks and enthusiasts who spend hours ploughing through deals and loopholes to accrue a massive amount of frequent flyer points, hotel upgrades and other perks.

It may also surprise you to find out that I am not yet one of these people. I really wish I had learned about travel hacking sooner, as I would have been accruing miles and reward points like crazy, given all the flying I've done and the places I've stayed.

To become a travel hacker you need dedication to doing a lot of ground-work, running a lot of numbers and keeping track of a lot of statistics. You also need a penchant for 'screwing' the system and sourcing intelligence.

If you don't fall into that category, don't worry. I'm going to cover some of the basic tips to get you started, and then bring in some heavyweight experts to give you the full lowdown. I also highly recommend Chris Guillebeau's Travel Hacking Cartel, designed to save you money on flights. It starts at $15 a month and is guaranteed to earn you at least four free plane tickets for every year you remain a member and apply what you've learned!

Miles are the new currency

"Miles and points are the primary way to get the most value from your travel. They are the new currency of travel, and when used properly can be more valuable than cash."

~ Steve Kamb, nerdfitness.com

According to Chris Guillebeau, earning reward miles falls into four categories: flying, ongoing promotions, seasonal promotions and special promotions. Interestingly, most miles are earned on the ground and not through flying.

Once you've earned miles, it's important that you put them to good use. You need to establish a goal for the miles you'll earn. Where will you go? How will you use them? As Chris says, miles are like money: a tool to give you more freedom and choice.

Here are some ideas:

- Get flights, hotel nights or better yet, both

- Lower the cost of your economy flights

- Get premium flights and upgrades to business or first class

- Get champagne service at beer budget rates

- Get cash back – usually on your credit card

- Transfer them to gift cards

- Buy merchandise.

Earning miles and points

Since miles and points are THE currency of travel hacking, you want as many points as you can possibly lay your hands on.

The following tips were gleaned from travel hacking experts Steve Kamb from Nerd Fitness, and Marvin Abisia from Intrepid Motion, when I attended their session on Travel Hacking at the World Domination Summit. Of course, I have added some of my own tips too.

Step 1: Join reward programs

You want to sign up for the major airlines' reward programs within the big three alliances.

1. **Oneworld**, consisting of American Airlines, British Airways, Cathay Pacific, Iberia, LAN, Qantas, and several others.

2. **Star Alliance** which consists of United, Continental, US Airways, Lufthansa, Swiss, and several more.

3. **Skyteam** which consists of Delta, Air France, KLM, and many others.

Step 2. Earn miles and points

After you've joined these programs then you need to get busy earning. Here are three key ways.

1. **Credit Cards:**

   The most points come from fantastic bonuses you get when signing up for a credit card. This can be anywhere from 25-100K points. The caveat is that you need to live in the US to get the full range of options.

   To put these points into perspective, 25,000 points are often enough to earn a free domestic flight, so within just a few weeks of having your card you can fly for free. Often though, these cards will have a minimum spend of between $500-$5,000 before the points are released. So simply use your card for almost every purchase, like gas, groceries, shopping, utilities, insurance, travel bookings and business expenses! (Always remember to pay off your card in full each month).

2. Point Exchanges:

Here, the strategy is to sign up for any and all offers from a merchant affiliated with the reward program. This can double or triple the number of miles you earn. For example, I recently earned 500 Virgin Elevate points simply by liking a Facebook page and entering my details.

3. Mileage Runs:

If you pay for a flight that's already a steal, you can still earn lots of points due to the mileage you rack up in the air.

Redeeming points for travel

This is the fun part. Reward tickets let you have a lot more flexibility than just a round-trip; often you can include a stopover too. This means you get better value for your miles.

There will be times when you're better off not using your reward points, especially if you can get a low-cost domestic flight for a bargain. Hold on to those precious points for longer, more expensive trips. For example, US Airways gets you to North Asia for 90,000 miles in business class, whereas on Delta that would be 170,000 miles.

Another thing to consider is that reward point bookings don't always work so well if you're in a hurry. It can take time to confirm them, your reward seats and routes may be limited and you could be better off just paying for your flights and using your credit card to earn more points for next time.

I recall flying a reward journey from London, UK, to Los Angeles, US, in 2012. It took me via Toronto and Philadelphia and was over 20 hours flying and transit time, compared to around 11 hours for a normal direct flight!

Here's a better example:

> "We had a super two weeks in Thailand that started with flying free on Thai Airways using our air miles, and then redeeming our points to stay free at Le Meridien Phuket. This was followed by another free four days stay at Le Meridien Khao Lak and an upgrade to a villa with our own attendant. We then enjoyed a week at the Bangkok Millenium Hilton for free and an upgrade to a giant room at the LAX Westin before heading home."
>
> ~ *Marcos Cristoforo Mercer*

Credit for flying high

Now you may be thinking that signing up for a bunch of credit cards to get amazing rewards points could put you in a lot of debt. Obviously that's a danger if you don't have a strategy. *The strategy is to always to pay the card off in full.*

Also be sure to cancel the ones you won't use anymore before the first year's annual fee. That said, it actually benefits your credit score to have a history of successful applications for credit, so keep old cards open that you've had for years, but with a zero balance.

Other things that impact your credit score are the number of on-time payments made, your total debt to total credit available, length of your credit history (age of each open credit card) and number of new credit card applications.

To minimize the hit on your credit score you want to do all your signups for new cards on the same day, every 90 days, depending on how serious a travel hacker you are. Keep your balances low, or better yet zero. You can monitor your credit rating using Credit Karma.

> "I flew from London via New York to Miami on Qantas using my points. I have had a Qantas Frequent Flyer (FF) membership forever and I also have a Visa and Amex card that I earn Qantas FF points with. I pay for everything with these two cards. I use Amex whenever there are no extra fees as I get double the points. I also find every opportunity to use partners for these cards like hire cars, retail stores, accommodation to earn extra points! I don't buy stuff for the sake of it only the things I need! "
>
> ~ *Kylie Pengelly, authenticfootprints.com*

Best credit cards

If you're in the US, you can apply for:

- **Chase Sapphire Preferred** with 40,000 bonus points if you spend $3,000 in first 3 months. This equates to $500 towards travel rewards. In fact, with one signup you'll have enough points for two round-trip flights in Economy Class within the US or one international flight.

- **Amex Starwood Preferred Guest** earns you up to 25,000 bonus Starpoints, 10,000 more after your first purchase and a further 15,000 after you spend $5,000 in 6 months of membership.

- **Citi Platinum Select** earns you 30,000 American Airlines AAdvantage® bonus miles after $1,000 in purchases within the first 3 months of card membership.

For a complete and up-to-date list of the best of the best then I highly recommend you check out Chris Guilleabeau's Cards For Travel site.

"Our trip to Thailand was one we will never forget. We found some-one to take care of our apartment, using AirBnB , who paid us $2,800 before we left.

"We booked our round trip tickets from San Francisco to Bangkok using free airline miles from our credit card and less than $45 in fees, saving us $16,000 on two ridiculously priced full-fare business class tickets (which we would never even consider buying).

"Once on the Island of Koh Lanta we decided to upgrade to the mod-est thatched roof bungalow, set over a small soft sandy beach cove. The cost of 4,050 Thai Baht included breakfast and wifi, which translates to just over $140 USD a night. We splurged because we had already made money from this trip."

~ Scott Dinsmore, liveyourlegend.net

Top tools for deals on travel and accommodation

There is no shortage of tools and services to book cheap flights and accom-modation, all designed to help travelers and entrepreneurs to travel smarter. However, it can get overwhelming, so I suggest you stick to using the best of the best, and cut out the rest. To get you started, I highly recommend you refer to the following two websites first, to plan your travel and then use the tools listed afterwards to actually book your trip.

TripAdvisor

TripAdvisor is the most useful tool for any traveler in my opinion. It gives you fantastic information about cities, countries, hotels, food, accom-modation and activities. Before you do anything, open up a tab on your browser for TripAdvisor. Then cross-reference any place you're thinking of booking in to, against the ratings and reviews of thousands of travelers before you make your decision.

TripIt

Create an account with TripIt and download the TripItPro application for your smartphone. It's a super simple way to organize all of your arrangements in one place. The app organizes accommodation and travel details into easy-to-see itineraries, and if a flight is delayed or a gate changes, it informs you by text or e-mail.

"The iPhone TripIt app is really cool. I use it to organize my flights, accommodation and transport. Say, for example, I purchase a flight for Brisbane to Cairns. I receive my confirmation email with the attached PDFs, and then simply forward them to plans@tripit.com. Within about 1 minute all those flight details are recorded and organized in my TripIt app, into my current travel plans. Effortlessly and easily. It's really quite ingenious."

~ *Kieran McDonogh*

Tools to book your flights

There are endless websites and services to book your travel. But if you really want to get savvy then choose from the three options below depending on your needs.

1. **DIY option:**

   My go-to tool of choice to book a flight is skyscanner.net, which is a great DIY aggregator of all the flight options across hundreds of airlines. Rather than opening up several browsers to search their travel aggregators, you just get one search result. What I like most is its accuracy.

   While I always advise you to check the local airlines in the country you're in to see if they have a better deal, nine times out of ten,

Skyscanner has found this for you. I also like the 'Everywhere' option if you want to see where you can fly to, anywhere in the world. They also have a mobile app where you can save your favorite searches. Two other options are Hipmunk and Airfarewatchdog.

2. Outsourcing option:

If you really don't have much time or inclination to search through results and book everything yourself, then outsourcing to flight search engine **Flightfox** is going to be right up your alley. You pay a fee, starting at US$24, and experts track down cheap flights for you. It's like having a really travel savvy Virtual Assistant do all the work for you. To get the best prices, you should do a quick search on Skyscanner first so that the Flightfox agents have a price to beat.

"I'm a fairly last-minute type of flier, and pretty savvy when it comes to finding my flights, but there is a gap between people like myself and the real flight hacking experts. While searching out a flight from Saskatoon, Canada (YXE) to Barcelona, Spain (BCN) I was hitting a dead end. Of the major flight searching services, Kayak was the best at $1149 for a one-way itinerary.

"Unhappy with what I found, I started a contest at Flightfox, where freelance "flight hackers" find you the best and cheapest flights. While travel agents have no incentive to search out the best deals for you, the experts at Flightfox compete to find the lowest price for you. I started a contest for $24 and gave them 72 hours to find the best deal and itinerary for me.

"Within hours, I was being sent itineraries that would already save me hundreds of dollars. In the end I had 4 choices given to me. I went with an itinerary that cost me $571, saving myself a cool $578 over Kayak thanks to their expertise of flight networks, charter companies and discount airlines. Perhaps the best $24 I've ever spent."

~ Dustin Main, toomanyadaptors.com

3. Old fashioned option:

I still think booking through a travel agent is a great option, particularly if you have a more complex itinerary in mind. They can do all the leg-work for you, especially on round-the-world trip tickets and packages, and you can sit down and ask them a ridiculous amount of annoying questions.

Their fee is usually built in and if you compare the price to your hourly charge it's most likely worth the money. Flight Centre is renowned for being an international travel agent with a great reputation.

At a pinch, call the airline direct, as the few agents that are still employed are seasoned veterans with a wealth of information and often have tricks that save you money. They have access to all inventories and often can work their magic to make the impossible possible.

Travel apps

Once you're done with all the flight bookings and accumulating your reward points to travel virtually for free, then make sure you check out and install the following apps for a smooth journey.

- **Flight Tracker** is the only free flight tracking and flight status app, which works with iPad, iPhone, Android, Blackberry, or Windows

- **Airport Transit Guide** is a traveler's complete guide to some 460 airports around the world, covering just about all the options for airport access – taxi, bus, rail, and shuttle – with fares, travel times, and pickup points, allowing you to make informed comparisons and money-saving decisions

- **Gate Guru** will help you navigate through unfamiliar airports so you're not left running to your gate.

Weather updates

Everyone talks about the weather for a reason – it can make or break a trip. If you didn't see the monsoon warning or realize that Japan was currently having a cold snap, you can arrive unprepared and it can ruin your experience. Usually you can use the weather app that comes with your smartphone or search online via Google. But the following two apps are handy to install and are more accurate:

- **Weather Channel** gives you the weather forecast, both local and international so you can plan ahead weeks, days or even hours.

- **Weather Bug** has more than 35,000 monitoring stations worldwide, so you can get access to super-local weather updates.

Getting around

What did we do before Google Maps and sophisticated navigation devices? Oh yeah, that's right, we used to read maps! I think you should aim to get a good sense of a place from looking at a map (either paper or online) and make a note of key spots in a new destination to get your bearings. However, you can also work with the following apps:

- **Google Maps**, online or via a smartphone app. It's free and you get turn-by-turn GPS navigation for driving, walking, public transport and sometimes bike routes. It also works when you're not connected to the Internet, if you've looked up the co-ordinates of your destination beforehand, as your smartphone's GPS still works without connection.

This is a lifesaver for me.

- **HopStop** gives you door-to-door public transit directions for subway, train, bus, ferry, bike & taxi for all of the US, Canada, UK, France, Australia, New Zealand and Russia.

- **Uber** acts as your private driver (in the US and Canada only, for now) and lets you request a ride at any time using your iPhone or Android.

- **MyTaxi** does the same and is a very cool app that shows reviews for your driver and their exact coordinates (available in Germany, Austria, Switzerland and branching into the US). You can also pay via your Smartphone and using PayPal.

- **WhatGas** allows you to find the cheapest prices on petrol or gas in several countries around the world. **Gas Buddy** works in Canada and the US.

Similar apps and services are popping up in more countries every day, so it helps to ask locals what they use and to try them out for yourself.

Budget accommodation options

Couchsurfing

Couchsurfing allows you to stay with hosts around the world for free. In return for staying with them, all that's usually required is to buy them a drink, a meal or to offer to clean up. With more than 1 million users in 70,000 cities, this service is big, and the word on the street is that, unless you're a regular user with lots of positive reviews, it is getting harder to be able to find a couch, as hosts are getting picky.

"Couchsurfing is a great way of exploring places on a budget without spending a lot of money on accommodation. Moreover, you can meet amazing people who can look after you and show you around the city. It's a great alternative for solo travellers not to feel lonely or for those who are looking for new friendship and fun. For me, Couchsurfing offers a chance to see the places from a local's perspective. I often ask my hosts to show me areas seldom visited by tourists, tell me some stories about their city and make me feel at home."

~ Agness Walewinder, etramping.com

Bizpora

BizSpora is like Couchsurfing or AirBnB but for entrepreneurs and independent business people, except it's more credible. They were formerly StartupStay.com, an invite-only platform and members were individually approved. Now it's open but they carefully monitor all new members. It's free to use, set up is easy and you can link it to your LinkedIn account. Simply search on a city you're traveling to, to see who's in that area and to view their profile and company.

If you like what you see you can contact them for coffee, or also to host you. As a user you can select whether you can host someone (you can charge for this) or just meet for coffee. Personally, I love this service and have used it in Amsterdam to receive two free day-passes to co-working spaces, meet the founders of a Startup Accelerator and host a friendly young French entrepreneur myself (as I actually had a place, for once).

Although it's more prevalent in Europe and North America, it's definitely growing and is a great way to connect with like-minded entrepreneurs when you reach a new city, opening up further opportunities.

Hostels

Hostels.com is a useful site, not only for hostels, but also for alternative lodgings, guesthouses, small hotels and private rooms per night. They list cheap eats, travel services and insurance options. You can also try hostelbookers.com and hostelworld.com

Universities

If you Google 'university dorm accommodation' in the city that you're looking at going to, you'll be surprised at how many dorm rooms are available, especially over the summer when the students are away. This is a legitimate option for affordable accommodation, especially in more expensive cities.

Home exchanges and house sitting

Just when you thought you had enough options, along comes yet another option for you. Do you fancy swapping houses with strangers, half way across the world, for a new adventure? Or perhaps you're a reliable house sitter? Check out these accommodation options that may suit your current situation:

Housesitting

Housesitting is essentially free accommodation, whereby you offer to look after a person's house while they go away. Sometimes you are required to maintain the place (like the garden) or even look after their pets. This can be for just a week, several months, or even a year or more. It's a great option to immerse yourself in an area and a culture, to work or study abroad, or to save money while you're trying to find your own house to buy.

You do usually need to register on a reputable site and have some references to show you're trustworthy. While there are many people looking to have house-sitters, it's a longer process to be accepted and make the arrangements, so this option does require some planning. Try MindMy-House.com with a $20 membership, or housesitworld.com or trusted-housesitters.com.

"In 2010 we put our things in storage and went on a traveling adventure without a plan. Within two months we stumbled across our first housesitting arrangement and for 10 months out of the next one and a half years we were caring for someone else's home and pets. We were even interviewed for an MSN article on housesitting, while we took care of the horses and house pets on this 24-acre property in the mountains.

"We are paid members of MindMyHouse.com and HomeCarers.com but found all of our housesitting opportunities through local classified ads, like craigslist.org and kijiji.com. As time goes on people begin to recommend you to friends and family, but in the beginning some persistence & friendly responses to requests will go a long way."

~ *Loralee Hutton, loraleehutton.com*

Home exchange

Vacation rental site Home Exchange claims you can travel anywhere and live for free and that over 250,000 people do this successfully every year. They offer exchanges for homes, condominiums and apartments, or hospitality exchanges, where you can host guests in your home, and then have the favor returned later.

The examples on their website are pretty cool, like the guy who traded his home for a 40ft yacht, or the couple who swapped their villa in Italy for an RV in Oregon, so that they could tour the US in true nomadic style.

"Home exchanging allows us to stay in other people's homes all round the world for free. We would be paying our mortgage on our apartment anyway, so this system lets us 'trade up' for weeks or months at a time without paying extra costs. Most times you can also exchange cars so you don't even have to pay car hire either.

"It works best for us to stay in homes because it's easier to run our business like this rather than staying in hotels. There are so many listings to choose from that we also always end up staying in amazing places- river side lodges, high rise luxury apartments, beach side cottages, pool villas, ski resorts!"

~ Hannah Alford, loveplaywork.com

You can also check out Intervac, the largest home exchange organization in the world, where you can choose from accommodation in over 50 countries. Or IHEN, which stands for the International Home Exchange Network and caters to home exchange and also vacation rentals.

Social media

No, I'm not joking by including this within budget accommodation options. It is a fantastic source for securing accommodation with friends, and friends of friends and even complete strangers. I get frequent emails from readers of my blog saying that if I ever come through their village, town or city, I have a place to stay. I've even taken some of them up on their offers.

These days our networks and extended networks really do allow us to tap into easy ways to connect with people, seeing their faces and photos, reading their profiles and working out if they're trustworthy. I sometimes search through my Facebook friends by location and then tell them that I'm coming to visit. Even if I don't stay with them, at least I get to catch up with them.

Often they'll suggest a friend who's happy to put me up for the night. This has worked especially well when I used to travel on a tight budget. You can search Twitter hashtags for locations, join LinkedIn travel groups and join Google+ communities too.

Mid-range budget accommodation options

If you fancy a step up from the budget accommodation, but don't require super fancy accommodation on your travels then you can find some great recommendations below. I've deliberately not included location-biased services (yes, I'm talking about those that only benefit Americans or those who travel within America). Once again there's such a huge range that I have wanted to focus on the best of the best.

Airbnb

Airbnb connects travelers with places to stay that aren't as expensive as hotels, and are more like renting your own apartment or house. Its focus is broader than vacation rentals. It has rooms, couches, homes, islands, castles and an airplane sticking out of a tree. You can browse through places in your price range, view photos, look at a map and read reviews. There's a fee involved when you book but it's worth it. You can also communicate with the property advertiser directly and ask questions before booking. Their response time is usually very fast.

Personally, I love Airbnb. I have used it to book a fantastic apartment in London, in a trendy area, for around £120 per night, as well as a small but well-located NYC apartment for around US $100, and a modern spacious 2-bedroom apartment in Bangkok for US $70 per night, which included a pool, tennis court and gym. Airbnb is continuing to expand its presence around the world so more locations are becoming available for you to choose from. It's also a handy place to advertise your own room, apartment or house when you're traveling and it's proving to be a lucrative revenue stream for many.

Agoda

Agoda is actually part of Priceline (which can be a hit or miss service, offering big discounts on hotels). I like it because it has global offers from more than 200,000 hotels worldwide (particularly great deals in Asia). I've had a lot of success in securing some incredible deals. In fact it's become a bit of a go-to resource for me. You earn reward points to apply to future accommodation bookings each time you book and leave reviews.

When I was staying in Cebu, I found a hotel which normally charged US$53, for $19 a night. What I like about Agoda is that it tells you how many rooms are left, who else is looking at the hotel and what else is in that area. It also provides a great map where you can hover over every single option in the location you're searching and see prices, ratings and click on reviews.

Expedia

This is the grandfather of the travel world and touts itself as the world's largest online travel agency. In my experience Expedia still has great search options and competitive deals. It's reputable and you can earn points each time you book, that you can then apply to future bookings for discounts.

Marketplace directories

Don't forget to check major directory listings like Craigslist and Kijiji for people renting out rooms, for short or long term lets, as well as people looking for roommates. These are often local prices so you can get some good deals, although it helps to be in the location you want to rent in, so that you can go and look at what's on offer. In the UK the best site is Gumtree.co.uk and in New Zealand it's Trademe.co.nz.

Group deal sites

When you know you'll be in one place for a while, sign up for Living Social or Groupon in the area and scout for deals. You can enjoy great deals on accommodation and often on city tours, museums and other tourist attractions.

This is perfect if you're staying for a few weeks or longer as you can seek out cheap hair cuts, a relaxing massage and even a gym membership for much less than normal. I did this while in Amsterdam where I visited gym after gym using offers, allowing me to discover all sorts of places I wouldn't have found otherwise (try it in your hometown too).

Luxury accommodation options

While I'd never say no to staying at a luxury resort or a 5 star hotel, it's not actually my style. I often find that associated with these places are overly fancy prices on nearby restaurants, bars and activities and they like to take advantage of the tourist's wallet.

You will witness this for yourself. While I was staying in a guesthouse in Batu Ferringhi beach, on Penang Island, I noticed that the prices in the high-end resorts for activities such as parasailing or jet skiing were three times the amount being charged in my local area

I get the feeling that people with serious money to spend probably aren't booking their own travel and many stays in top hotels and accommodation is organized through private referrals and connections, and these people are unlikely to be reading my book. In case you're going to treat yourself, or upgrade your travels, Leading Hotels of the World are accepting members.

Eating out

For foodies who adore tasting the local cuisine and discovering the best spots, nothing beats asking the locals for their recommendations, especially restaurants and cafés not on the tourist trail. Here are some apps and services to help otherwise:

- **Yelp** comes in handy to look up what places are around you based on category of venue, cuisine, price or proximity. You also get user reviews and recommendations, and a quick search interface for address and phone numbers.

- **Foodspotting** is one of the easiest ways to find and share the foods you love with other food lovers.

Internet and Wi-Fi

Until the day you can't connect or get decent Wi-Fi, you will never realize how much you depend upon it. In fact, I'd say that losing connection is the bane of every traveling entrepreneur's life! Trying to get decent Internet connection has cost me way too much time and money over the years.

It's also taught me patience and to do as much work offline as possible, especially in countries where the bandwidth is next to useless. Do your research in advance. If you're heading somewhere with notoriously bad, expensive or slow Internet then I'd recommend scheduling calls, interviews and major file uploads for another time.

Luckily I've done that research for you by looking at Akamai's State of the Internet report for Q1 2013, where you can find countries ranked on their broadband speeds every quarter.

Top 10 countries for fastest Internet

Hong Kong comes in first place, with an average peak connection speed of 54.1Mbps. At that speed you can download an entire feature film in just a few minutes!

Next is South Korea (48.8 Mbps), which is way more affordable than other Western countries. People in Seoul can get 100 megabit-per-second lines for $31.90 a month.

In third place is Japan (42.2 Mbps), then Latvia (37.5 Mbps), Romania (37.4 Mbps), Belgium (32.7 Mbps), Switzerland (32.4 Mbps), Bulgaria (32.1 Mbps), Israel (30.9 Mbps) and in 10th place is Singapore (30.7 Mbps). In case you're wondering, the US is 14th place at 29.6 Mbps.

Free Wi-Fi – pros and cons

You can access free Wi-Fi throughout most of the first world, and that's only going to continue to increase. In second and third world countries, you take what you can get.

If you can't access the Internet from the airport, your accommodation or cafés, you can still find those things called 'Internet cafes'. The upsides of having Wi-Fi constantly available are that you can work from "almost anywhere", for free, and this gives you unbelievable flexibility in running your business, staying in touch and making money.

The downside is that most Wi-Fi signals are unencrypted. This means that anything you do online in hotels, coffee shops and airports can be intercepted by others using the same network. That's why it pays not to login to online banking or other important sites through an unsecured network, to protect yourself from being hacked. Even anti-virus software won't keep you safe from this.

"When we were at the Portland Airport last year, we used their open (no password) Wi-Fi network to pay for our tickets to the World Domination Summit using PayPal. I had just enough time to complete the transaction and didn't think much about it. When we touched down in Berlin the next day, I saw all these emails from PayPal for "Postal Service Payments."

"I logged into PayPal and saw that there was over $2,000 charged to our account. With the open Wi-Fi network, someone had been able to hack into my account. It looked like the hacker had done one payment of $150 to test the waters and when he saw that I didn't respond (because I was on a flight) he just kept going. Fortunately, PayPal recognized it as fraud immediately and refunded the money. Lesson learned: never do any financial transactions over an unsecured Wi-Fi network!"

~Audrey Scott, uncorneredmarket.com

The other thing is that free Wi-Fi can mean an unreliable connection. I have too many examples to share of the great lengths I've gone to, in order to make things happen when there's poor or intermittent Internet. I remember sitting in a campsite in the remote west coast of the South Island of New Zealand, trying to get a signal to start a webinar. I had just enough connection time to introduce my guest, before I lost connectivity. Luckily I'd given him the webinar controls in advance.

Another time was when I was in an Internet Café in a small village in Sarawak, Borneo, trying to upload my video for the Kickstarter campaign for this book. It took 6 hours and 32 minutes to upload, only to fail at the last moment, because one too many 'gamers' came in, reducing the bandwidth big time. My patience was close to evaporating until I remembered this was the life I chose and as a result, moments like these are to be expected.

Here are three tools to help you find and take advantage of free Wi-Fi

- **Free Wi-Fi Finder** lets you search for free Internet Hotspots anywhere in the world, both online and off.

- **Skype Wi-Fi** allows you to get online at over 1 million Wi-Fi hotspots worldwide and only pay for the time you're online with Skype Credit. You just need the latest version of Skype or their Wi-Fi app.

- **What's App** is a free app you install on your smartphone that allows you to text message anyone for free and send photos when you have Wi-Fi or data connection.

Of course it helps if you have a data package on your smartphone to start with, so that you can actually use the handy apps mentioned here and not have to search for free Wi-Fi all the time.

These apps are especially useful when you don't have your laptop, and instead rely on your smartphone to check emails, social media or maps. Be sure to try out:

- **DOODAD.** This is a data-only travel SIM card, which you put into your unlocked smartphone or tablet, to gain access to pre-paid data (which lasts a year). You can use it in over 50 countries, and counting. For up-to-date rates and countries (and to order your own) visit their website.

If you're wondering about texting and calls, those aren't a feature, but that's why you use WhatsApp and Skype!

Private Wi-Fi

Wi-Fi hotspots at hotels, airports and coffee shops are likely to be your lifeline to getting the job done when you're on the road. But even though hotspots have revolutionized the way we work when we travel, they're not secure.

If you're concerned about the privacy and security of your sensitive information, Private Wi-Fi is a virtual private network service (VPN) that encrypts your communications, making them invisible to hackers and creating a private tunnel within any public Wi-Fi network.

Once you download the software, you can do whatever you like online in a secure environment (with bank level encryption). There are versions for laptops (PCs and Macs) as well as tablets and phones (Android and iOS). So no matter what devices you use, your online personal and business communications are protected anywhere in the world. It's certainly worth the monthly US$10 subscription fee.

Protecting your valuables

Being pick-pocketed or having your valuables stolen while traveling sucks, but it is going to happen to you at some point. So here are a few simple ways to protect your valuables, aside from the insurance that I've covered already, and the key tools I mentioned for backup and protection in Chapter 7.

Smartphone security

If you've spent enough money on a device that allows you to run your business and your life from your hand, it pays to protect that device from the start. It's important that you take time to secure your smartphone device when you buy it, or get someone to show you how. This will be the best investment of five minutes of your time.

iPhone security hacks

If you own an iPhone then you want to ensure you have put a passcode lock on it, at the very minimum. You should enable regular back-ups to iCloud which is a free feature offered by Apple, as well as enabling Find My iPhone. Make sure your "Location Services" is set to 'on' and your date and time is correct.

That said, muggers and thieves aren't exactly tech idiots and they can just *turn off your location services* to make it impossible to find your phone. So make sure you change your privacy settings under "Restrictions" to enable a privacy passcode and also select "Don't Allow Changes" under location option in your privacy settings.

Here, you are basically delaying the person who stole your phone from disabling your location service until the police can help you track it down. Once you've enabled Find My iPhone, you can navigate to Restrictions to stop others deleting applications too.

Android security hacks

There are so many different Android devices that it pays to check the specific security options you can enable. Either ask the store assistant to show you how or Google the instructions.

According to many reviews online TrustGo Antivirus & Mobile Security is the best free app to secure your Android. It has an impressive amount of features including a privacy guard, backup option and anti-theft tools for locating your missing phone and remotely wiping it. You can get it from the Google Play store.

Laptop protection

The day your laptop gets stolen with all its precious data like photos, videos, files and other important data you've been storing for years, you'll wish you had taken better precautions. So here are two simple things to do today to protect your machine:

1. Password protect your computer to prevent anyone from just logging in when it's already on. Have a timer set for 10 minutes of activity that then locks your computer when it's not in use. Once again check, out the key tools and precautions I cover in Chapter 7 for your online business activities.

2. Install Prey from Prey Project, a feature-rich and stable open-source program, on your laptop. It's free and puts all the paid software to shame with the amount of fancy features it includes like Wi-Fi auto-connect, GPS and Wi-Fi geo-location, small memory footprint, webcam and screenshot capture, remote data removal and will lock down your PC.

"A friend I met here while living in Costa Rica told me about Prey Project and how this software helped him, with the assistance of local police, recover his stolen MacBook Pro. It's a free piece of software that takes snapshots of activity on whatever device you have it installed on. In his case, he got actual photos of, not the guy that stole it, but of people who bought the stolen MacBook. I'd recommend installing this on all your devices, I have."

~ *Susan Whitehead, familytravelbucketlist.com*

Obviously common sense counts for a lot when you're traveling. If you don't see people flashing their phones or laptops in cafés, as a general rule of thumb, keep yours hidden from view. Don't leave your valuables alone or out of eyesight and choose bags and cases that don't scream 'I'm a sexy laptop, pick me'.

When I was biking through Malawi in Africa for example, I never took out my laptop in a public area, as I knew it would literally draw crowds. I also took a simple touchtone phone with me, which I didn't care if I lost, instead of my iPhone. Contrast that with South Korea where everyone has the latest gadgets and devices and is showing them off, almost as a pastime.

Travel accessories

When it comes to handy accessories that make your life on the road easier, you want to keep in mind that less is best, and lighter is definitely more practical. It seems that the Swiss are particularly innovative on this front and have made some of the best accessories I've ever used. While they're not always cheap, they are beautifully designed and built to last.

The tools I recommend next are more to do with making your life easier when it comes to running your business from anywhere. I go for durability and reliability when it comes to travel tools, so here are my top recommendations.

Adaptor

The one tool I can't live without, as a Suitcase Entrepreneur, aside from my laptop and passport, is a travel adaptor. There is nothing worse than sitting for hours in airports or bus stations with your electronic devices out of battery life.

My recommendation is the SKRoss World Adapator Pro + USB. It's sexy, sleek and lightweight and includes six different country plugs. You can find the right connection for anywhere in the world, and charge two USB devices at the same time. You're also guaranteed a safe power connection in more than 150 countries on all continents.

Multi-tool adaptor

At some point you'll lose the charger or cable for your iPhone or smartphone, which is highly frustrating. That's why I really like the Lifetrons High Tech Multi-Tool Adaptor. It looks like a Swiss Army knife and synchronizes and charges your mobile devices with your computer simultaneously. What's even cooler is that it has a built-in SIM card holder and viewing stand for watching videos. It works with your iPod, iPhone, iPad and most micro and mini USB devices.

Power charger

Normally, if you're prepared, you'll have all your devices charged before you hit the road, but there are always delays, extended layovers and airports or stations that just don't have power sockets available. It's in these moments when you wish you had a back-up power supply to do your work, and an extra set of outlets.

"One of my most important accessories is also the simplest and cheapest. I picked up a generic 4-way power box at the local hardware store a couple of days before leaving on my trip, and barely a day goes by where I don't use it.

Power sockets are always in short supply, whether I'm staying in a hotel, guesthouse or dorm room. Also, most of my tech gear has Australia/NZ plugs on it, which are of precisely zero use outside those two countries. Rather than carrying multiple travel adapters, I can plug all of my chargers into my cheap little power box, the box into a single travel adapter and the adapter into the wall.

As a final bonus, the cord on the power box acts as a short extension cable for the inevitable times that the one available plug is behind the bed or halfway up a wall. The thing cost about five bucks, but as a traveller, it's worth its weight in gold.

~ Dave Dean, whatsdavedoing.com

Portable power charger

When there's no power to be found at all, your devices are running low on power and you need them for the next leg of your journey, then you need a portable power pack. This is such a handy tool for a Suitcase Entrepreneur. Here are my top recommendations

- **Lifetrons High Performance Digital Power Charger** claims to be the world's smallest high capacity portable charger that you can use with your smartphones, mobile phones and tablets. It has dual USB ports so you can charge two devices at once, and the fancy, integrated power-saving and safety technology, provides around 15-20 days' power to a mobile phone, around 30 days for an iPhone 4 (on standby mode).

- **Anker® Astro Pro2 20000mAh External Battery Charger** can power your tablet, netbook, notebook, laptop and smartphone. It's compatible with HP, Dell, Acer, Asus, Toshiba Notebooks, Google Nexus Tablets, iPads, iPhones, Samsung Galaxy S4, S3, and Note 2.

- **Powerbag Business Class Pack** is the ultimate wearable solution, as a backpack with a built-in battery system that has enough power to charge your average smart-phone, up to 4 times. It comes with handy padded laptop and tablet pockets with a "Checkpoint Friendly" FlyFlat design, which apparently means you don't need to remove your laptop or tablet from the bag when you're going through airport security.

- **Mophie Juice Pack Plus** is a really cool, fully protective, form-fitting case with an extended, built-in rechargeable battery for your iPhone and the PowerSkin Protective Case with Built-in Battery does the same for Motorola DROID X and DROID X2.

External hard drive

Even if you're using Dropbox or AmazonS3 to store all your important files in the cloud, there's no harm in having an external hard drive too. This is especially handy when you have terrible Internet connection and syncing your files on your computer is going to take hours. Make sure that you store your hard drive in a separate place from your laptop, just in case one gets stolen.

Hard drives have come a long way from the days where you had to spend a lot of money for not much memory. The good news is, they're getting faster, cheaper and more lightweight every year. My two recommendations are:

1. **Seagate Backup Plus** is what I currently use, complete with 1TB of memory and USB 3.0 port. It has a handy one-click custom back up plan that you can schedule for weekly full back-ups by simply connecting it to your laptop. It also enables user-generated content to be backed up from your favorite social network or shared directly to them.

2. **My Passport Essential SE** offers you a 1 TB size as well as 750GB, which is more than ample to store a ton of stuff. It's a complete powerhouse, with fast speeds and a super slim profile, perfect for traveling light. It also has both USB 2.0 and USB 3.0 ports, so as you upgrade your laptop, this hard drive will still be up to date. For under US$70 it's a steal.

Luggage scale

This isn't a necessity unless you're constantly pushing the luggage weight restrictions, or perhaps traveling where there is limited carry on and cabin weights you have to adhere to. Use this tool to weigh your bag(s) before you reach the airport and get hit with excess luggage charges. Your wallet will thank you for it. The bestselling recommendation is the EatSmart Precision Voyager Digital Luggage Scale. You just hang your luggage on the hand-held scale to see how heavy it is, up to 50kg or 110lbs.

Anti-jetlag drink

While it's not technically a tool or an app, you're going to appreciate 1Above. This is your inflight drink to cure or decrease jetlag, especially on those long-haul flights. They come in handy travel-sized 100ml concentrates, which you just add to water when on the plane. It will keep you hydrated and better able to cope with the change in time zones.

Language learning tools

With so many free resources online there's no shortage of apps and software you can use. Listening to podcasts is a great way to go, as you can bring them with you and they take up no space in your luggage! You can download language learning podcasts or podcasts in different languages to get used to listening to a normal spoken speed. Try Espanol Podcast, Daily French Pod, Learn Italian Pod, My German Class and Learn Chinese Pod to name but a few.

> "When you have the basic phrases down, then a good beginner's course could be Teach Yourself. Other completely free language learning resources include: Duolingo, Memrise, Learning With Texts, Tunein for live streaming radio, Wordreference for a much better word specific dictionary than Google Translate, and my favourite App is Anki for spaced repetition flashcards with a pre-made database of language specific decks you can download."
>
> *~Benny Lewis, Fluent In Three Months*

Of course we could geek out on all sorts of fun and funky travel tools and services but, at the end of the day, you only have so much room in your suitcase and less is more, as you well know. Over time, and as your travel style changes and adapts, you will work out the best tools, accessories and services for your unique needs.

Take these actions to fly for free and travel smarter

- Start educating yourself on the rules of travel hacking and use the recommendations in this chapter to accrue points and rewards from now on

- Try out Flightfox and run a contest on a complex journey to see the savings you can make

- Use one of the methods of finding free accommodation or great deals and then challenge yourself to beat the costs of living at home

- Download the appropriate applications that you will find most handy and then actually use them!

- Check out some of the cool and useful tools suggested and let me know which ones make your life easier. You can view them all at **suitcaseentrepreneur.com/book/resources** Chapter 13.

Conclusion

Choosing freedom in business and adventure in life.

You have brains in your head. You have feet in your shoes. You can steer yourself any direction you choose. You are on your own. And you know what you know. And YOU are the one who'll decide where to go. … Will you succeed? Yes, you will indeed! (98 and 3/4 percent guaranteed.) Kid, you'll move mountains.

~DR. SEUSS

While it's entirely possible to run your business and make money from a beach (and I have), what we're really talking about in this book is freedom.

Freedom to do what you want, when you want, with whoever you want, from anywhere you want.

To achieve this you need to work hard, hustle and be determined to stick it out for the long haul. You have to be willing to take risks and you have to persist in seeing your vision become a reality.

There is no such thing as easy money and nothing worth doing was ever easy. But, if you're prepared to work smart and develop a laser-like focus on achieving your ideal lifestyle, then anything is possible.

The truth is that you choose your own reality

As you have read, I am set on living my life by these values – ***creating freedom in business and adventure in life.***

I use my profits to buy experiences that enrich my life and invest back into those lives of people who I care about and want to help achieve their ideal lifestyle.

If you're like me and other location-independent freedom seekers, then you work smart. You create systems that work for you and make you more efficient, so that you can work on what you love doing more often.

You choose where to travel next based on whether that makes you feel happy, energized and alive. Sometimes you do it for the challenge or the adventure and sometimes because it's practical.

You are equally as comfortable sleeping on the floor or a couch as you are staying in a swanky five-star hotel, because in reality it's the company you keep, the people you meet and the attitude you choose that counts, in business and in your personal life. It's the things money can't buy that truly make you feel lucky to be alive.

Life is about making the most of every single moment, not wasting time stuck in a situation you hate, but instead choosing to live your best life by doing what you love that also makes you money and improves other people's lives.

There is no such thing as a 4-hour work week

Really, there isn't. I'll tell you why. If you love what you do, and you want to create meaning in the work you do and make a difference in the world, you'd never want to squeeze it into just four hours a week,

Tim Ferriss, an American author, entrepreneur, angel investor, and public speaker, inspired hundreds of thousands of people to view life differently, including me. He published the 4-Hour Workweek back in 2007 and what he wrote about still holds true.

The fundamental message of Tim's book is that you don't have to choose the cookie-cutter life that society maps out for you. You can work less than a standard 35-hour week and outsource yourself so that you can focus on the work that holds real meaning for you.

I believe you should choose to spend your hours on this earth pushing yourself to live your best life and constantly innovating, producing, shipping and achieving as well as having a ton of fun. Just know what your ideal lifestyle is and then set your goals to head towards it each and every day.

Money is not the be all and end all

I feel rich, yet I'm not – not in the sense that other people would call me rich. Money can buy you independence, it can buy you a sense of freedom, it can buy you a whole lot of things that you don't *really* need (property, fancy cars, designer clothes, kitchen gadgets, extra shoes, the latest gimmicks). But money cannot buy you happiness.

The truth is that happiness comes from within. It comes from accepting that, without all manner of material possessions, titles and status, you are just another human being who loves, eats, sleeps and shits like everyone else does. The best thing you can have in life is your health, your happiness and your loved ones.

So use this book to build a profitable business that allows you to live a meaningful life and ensure others around you do the same.

Having no fixed abode isn't always that sexy

Living in different countries, travelling when you feel like it, cruising the world on a yacht, booking out an island resort to party with your friends all sounds pretty awesome. To be fair, those things are the major benefits to being location independent and designing your own lifestyle.

It really is fantastic to know that you can work from anywhere you choose to. What people tend to dismiss though, is that living out of a suitcase, a backpack or having no home base is not for the faint hearted. That's why you need to choose your level of location independence that's right for you. That's what this book was for.

Constant travelling is about the challenge of setting up in a new location, learning new languages, discovering rich cultures and new value systems. It is about figuring out what to do when the local bank doesn't recognize your bank cards or when the local restaurant won't serve you a vegetarian meal or when you're left stranded in a location due to a transport issue that you have no idea about.

Having no fixed abode also means you appreciate what you have when you're back home with friends and family, and being grateful for what you do have in life when you visit places where they have so little.

So welcome to your new life as a Suitcase Entrepreneur

Once you can tick the boxes below then you are going to enjoy a lifestyle where you choose your own adventure:

- You are a citizen of the world, not bound to material obsessions

- You seek new ways of working while embarking on adventures.

- You are equally as happy to be working your own hours from a far away destination, or from your favorite café just five minutes down the road.

- You are driven by a need to do more with your life, and in a way that fits your notion of what really living life means to you.

- Your eyes light up when you describe your passion for what you do, how much you love your life as location independent digital entrepreneur.

- You have the right mindset and sense of the fulfillment you desire.

Being a Suitcase Entrepreneur is about doing what's important to you. It's about having more of your perfect days in an average week, until one day you wake up and realize you're living your ideal lifestyle, exactly as you envisioned it.

Freedom by choice

You have the right to live your life how you want to, without sitting in endless meetings, getting stuck in long commutes and having to be in one location in order to run a successful business and ultimately to enjoy their life.

As you have read, the future of work is such that the humble office will be a thing of the past. Technology and online tools are smarter, faster and cheaper than ever and it is entirely possible to start a business for as little as $100.

Travel has become so much affordable and the world has become increasingly more accessible. There's virtually no place in the world you can't visit and discover. Location, time zones and languages are no longer barriers to building a mobile business that has a truly global reach from your laptop or smartphone.

The intangible benefits of being a Suitcase Entrepreneur can only be explained when you truly live this lifestyle yourself. I adore the lifestyle business I've created for myself. You will too.

I hope that through this book, I have opened the doors to your imagination on how you can achieve a similar level of freedom for yourself today, by taking action and applying this to your own life to make your dream lifestyle a reality.

Resources

Your go-to directory.

You can use this mini-summary section to refer back to as a quick-reference tool for any resource I've mentioned throughout the book – such as checklists, downloads, books, websites, apps, tools and services.

Your best bet is to head to **suitcaseentrepreneur.com/book/resources** to find the most up to date list of resources at anytime and downloadable templates.

Chapter 1:

- Look at the Sweet Spot diagram and take time to work out yours

- **FundRazr** (the fundraising application for Facebook that the company I co-founded built)

- **BYOB Build Your Online Business** guide

Chapter 2:

- Watch **Randy Pausch's Last Lecture**

- Learn more about minimalism at **Becoming Minimalist.**

- **Read great articles or pick up a copy of Sell Your Crap** from Man vs Debt

Chapter 3:

- Case Studies include:

- Sean Ogle **Location 180**.

- Jodi Ettenburg's **Legal Nomads**

- Colin Wright **Exile Lifestyle**

- Dan Andrew **Lifestyle Business Podcast**

- Daryl Mander **Digital Marketing Consultant**

- Leanne Pittsford and Leah Neaderthal **Start Somewhere**

- Full Tilt Author **Rebekah Tyler**

- Greg and Rachel Denning **Discover Share Inspire**

- Hannah and Chris Alford **Love Play Work**

- Full-Time Adventurer **Dave Cornwaithe**

- Natural Horse Coach **Geneviève Benoit**

- AJ and Melissa Leon **Pursuit of Everything**

Chapter 4:

- **Viewsy** geo-targeting and location based service for retailers

- **Mist.io** B2B service to manage and monitor your virtual machines across clouds

- **Bableverse** offers an on-demand voice translation service by pro interpreters and bilinguals, in any language and situation.

- **CLYC** has produced the first digital bicycle lock

- **Google Wallet** for digital online payments

- **Trustev** is a real-time, online verification for shopping online that uses social fingerprinting technology

- **How to Fund Your Dream Idea on Kickstarter.**

- **Fast Forward Your Business** by Roger Hamilton

- **ShoutEm** and **Bizness Apps** mobile App Making tools

- **iBuildApp** is a fully functional platform allowing you to create a catalogue, magazine or an iPad app

- **Newsstand** is a service provided by Apple to allow you to easily and simply deliver magazine and newspaper content via free or paid subscription.

- **Magzter** offers service as Newsstand but focuses on foreign titles and the growing base of Android-based tablets.

- **Google Fiber** is an Internet and cable solution.

- **Kindle Publishing** allows you to self-publish books and your blog.

- **YouTube** lets you to Start with a YouTube Channel and broadcast yourself.

- **Animoto** is a great tool that takes your photos and videos and turns them into professional videos

- **Ezvid** allows you to both record your screen and edit the video.

- **Screencast** is great too and it's good for both MAC and PC.

- **PayPal's app** lets you send and receive payments from your mobile

- **Square** has really led the way on the payments front.

- **Square Terminal** turns your iPad into a cash register.

- **iZettle** offers an app to install and a miniature card reader

- **Bitcoins** digital online currency

- **Ripple** acts as a global system for making transactions of any kind, be it US dollars, Euros.

- '**Create Awesome Online Courses**' by David Siteman Garland

- Futurists and big picture thinkers: **Ray Kurzweil** (technology), **Khan Academy** (education), **Virgin Galactic** (space travel), **Oliver Bussmann** (the global workforce) and **Dr. Gene Robinson** (global climate).

- **LeadPages** is the easiest way to create beautiful landing pages, launch pages, sales pages and squeeze pages for your website that actually convert.

Chapter 5:

- **CreativeLIVE** and **Udemy** live video-course platforms

- Sean Rodgers **Prime8Movement**

- Britta Wein **Lunapads.de**

- Prerna Malik **Social Media Direct**

- Pat Flynn **Smart Passive Income**

- **The $100 Startup** from Chris Guillebeau

- **Start a Freedom Business** from Colin Wright

- **Click Millionaires** by Scott Fox

Chapter 6:

- **OurDeal** online contract tool

- **Bidsketch** freelance proposal software

- **Bloomberg study on best countries to do business**

- **Business requirements in the EU**

- **Economy rankings based on ease of doing business**

- **Global tax links**

- **Kyle Durand's site**

Chapter 7:

- **Google Everything** — Gmail, Google Docs, Google Calendar, Google Apps – emails, online shared documents, drafts, forms, and scheduling

- **MS Office** or **OpenOffice** – for all your writing and presentation and spreadsheet needs

- **NeatDesk** designed for a real office to gain back both valuable office space and time lost searching for information in inefficient, outdated filing cabinets.

- **Grasshopper** as your virtual entrepreneur phone system people can reach you on, complete with voicemail.

- **Skype Personal Number** is a simple solution for your own number and voicemail capability.

- **Google Voice** for US only.

- **Dropbox** cloud storage solution. **AmazonS3** is an alternative

- **Bitrix24** which is like Yammer (social enterprise) plus BaseCamp (project management) plus Zoho (CRM) plus DropBox, plus Skype and a few minor things (calendars, planners, work reports, Gantt charts, etc) all rolled into one.

- **Shoeboxed** lets you send receipts, business cards and documents to them via postage-paid envelopes or camera-equipped smartphone

- **Freshbooks** is your financial accounting and invoicing system, time and expense tracker and perfect for managing your clients and contractors.

- **Xero** online accounting software is a full-featured web based system for invoicing, accounts payable, bank reconciliation & bookkeeping.

- **Indinero** is a real-time dashboard for your business' finances to allow you to focus on the big picture of your financial health.

- **Hostgator** allows you to choose from a range of website hosting plans and deliver a variety of services including setting up your own website.

- **Namecheap** offer some of the most affordable domain names in the industry, in addition to full-featured web hosting packages.

- **WordPress** is web software you can use to create a beautiful website or blog and manage your online content

- **LeadPages** is the easiest way to create beautiful landing pages, launch pages, sales pages and squeeze pages for your website that actually convert.

- **Optimize Press** lets you build customized marketing landing pages, but more importantly membership sites to host your programs and courses.

- **Hootsuite** is your all-in-one social media dashboard that allows you to post and schedule updates to multiple social media platforms at once, as well as track keywords, hashtags, lists and your analytics.

- **Tweet Adder** automates your repetitive tweeting tasks, gets you more followers and generally saves you time.

- **Mailchimp** allows you to design and send beautiful emails, manage your subscribers and track your campaign's performance. Equal alternative is **Aweber.**

- **InfusionSoft** is a robust solution to really turn your business into a serious sales and marketing machine, as well as handle email management and lead generation

- **WiseStamp** email signature tool that transforms your boring email into clever branding for your business. You can link your social media profiles, blog feed, videos and more into your signature or sell products.

- **MeetingBurner** is a great webinar and online meeting platform that you can use to present to many or one, record video and audio and capture leads

- **AdRoll** is an effective retargeting platform to allow your ads to be seen in all the right places based on your ideal customer. **Perfect Audience** is a retargeting platform for Facebook.

- **PayPal** business or premium account lets you link your bank account and credit card and is the easiest way to set up payments for goods and services.

- **e-Junkie** lets you sell your digital products and programs for a $5 per month fee

- **Gumroad** lets you sell directly with a link, you don't even need a website or PayPal account. Great for creatives selling their goods.

- **Zoho CRM** gives you a 360-degree view of your complete sales cycle and pipeline so you can keep track of your existing and potential clients, leads and sales opportunities too.

- **Zendesk** is a cloud based customer serviced software that takes customer communication from anywhere—your website, email, phone, Twitter, Facebook, and chat—and turns it into a ticket for you and your support team to deal with.

- **Wufoo** lets you create customized and branded professional feedback forms and surveys. Google Forms does the job too but with less pizazz.

- **Google Hangouts** are a great way to hold live group calls with customer and clients for tutorials, Q&A or focus groups.

- **Google Analytics** for tracking critical website and traffic data

- **Google Alerts** and **Postrank** social mention monitoring tools

- **oDesk** and **Elance** are your go-toonline workforce communities for hiring competent freelancers or permanent virtual staff to get the job.

- **OurDeal** great for creating, sending and electronic signing of agreement and contracts within seconds

- **Bidsketch** allows you to customize proposals for clients (especially freelancers), cutting down the time you spend preparing them and using digital delivery and signoff.

- **Hello Fax** is a digital faxing solution that stops the need for you to have an office and from having to download attachments, print them, sign them and fax them.

- **LastPass** allows you to store all your passwords safely and securely in one location, as well as important data like bank accounts with just one password.

- **Asana** is a free project and team management tool that allows you to create projects and assign and track tasks, leave notes, links, upload documents.

- **Rapportive** is a handy app that works right inside Gmail, giving you a real time report of who the person emailing is including their name, picture, location, company and social media accounts.

- **SaneBox** takes unimportant emails out of your Inbox, puts them in a separate folder, and aggregates them into a daily summary so you can focus on what's important.

- **Evernote** allows you to organize your thoughts, web clippings and notes into an handy cloud storage system that syncs across devices

- **ScheduleOnce** is a meeting and appointment scheduling software that increases customer satisfaction, creates a smooth process for clients, and saves you messing with international time-zone confusion-

- **RescueTime** is a productivity tracking tool you install on your device. It monitors your every move and then shows detailed reports about what you spent your time on and where you can optimize your current routines to save an average of 3.5 hours a week

- Checkout my definitive list of tools page on my website that's constantly being updated at **suitcaseentrepreneur.com/tools**

Chapter 8:

- **2013 Social Media Marketing Industry Report** by Social Media Examiner

- Cheryl Wood, **MoonlightCreativeWorks.com**

- Natalie MacNeil, **SheTakesOnTheWorld.com**

- Search on **search.twitter.com**

- Kirsten Hodgson **Kaleidoscope Marketing**

- Filipe Dinis' **DesignHandyMan**

- Karl Staib, **Domino Connection**

- **Google Alerts** is a free service that allows you to enter relevant keywords or phrases you're interested in.

- **Viralheat** covers every corner of the social web from Facebook, Twitter, Real-time web, to YouTube and lets you know your social media mentions.

- **Klout** shows how influential you are across the social networks and gives you an aggregate score of how much clout you have in your area of expertise (based upon your fans and followers), compared to others.

- Come hang with me on Twitter **@suitcasepreneur** or connect with me on **Facebook** or **Google Plus** as a start.

Chapter 9:

- **oDesk** and **Elance** outsourcing platforms

- **Jing** and **MeetingBurner** for online screen-sharing videos and meetings

- Tina Forsyth, author of Becoming an Online Business Manager' and **The Entrepreneur's Trap**

- Chris Ducker's **Virtual Staff Finder** service

- **Zendesk** customer service platform

- **Hiremymom.com** is a popular site, particularly for those wanting office managers and assistants who are trustworthy.

- **99designs** and **Crowdspring** for specific design work like websites, logos and branding.

- **fiverr.com** community of freelancers doing small tasks for $5

- **Mechanicalturk** is a service provided by Amazon, which is great for entrepreneurs and developers who need small "human intelligence tasks" done

- **Microtask** is a platform for real-time and scalable on-demand outsourcing.

- **How to Create Freedom in Business** Slideshare presentation on my Painted Picture

Chapter 10:

- **TeuxDeux** simple to-do list tool

- **Freedom** for MAC or **Leechblock** Firefox extension block out all distracting sites

- **Schedule Once** online calendar booking service

- **timeanddate.com** to figure out your time zone differences

Chapter 11:

- **G Adventures 2013 survey**

- Trip Advisor's **Traveler's Choice of 2013**

- **$100 Change program**

- **Piktochart** infographic tool

- **Skyscanner.net** flight booking service

- **Zufall dice** to help you make your next decision on where you next go

- Lessons on relationships, **Mike Hrostoski**

- **Visa requirements**

- **Vaccinations**

- **Political stability**

- **Electricity supply**

- **Lonely Planet's online travel resources**

- **World Nomads travel insurance**

Chapter 12:

- Joshua Becker, **Becoming Minimalist**

- **The Travel Doctor** for medical resources and vaccinations

- **OneSimCard** *is an International SIM card* with free incoming calls in 150 countries and outgoing calls priced from $0.25/min and data from $0.20/MB

- **GoSim** has international SIM cards from $19, with cheap calls from 29c per min. and data from 49c per MB, and with coverage in 185 countries.

- **WorldSIM** allows you to make and receive international calls on your mobile without incurring expensive charges.

- **SpareOne,** the only mobile phone that you can use anywhere in the world.

- **TripAdvisor** for travel recommendations and planning

- **Agoda.com or Booking.com** for good accommodation deals.

- **italki.com** for free language exchanges or very affordable private lessons

- **Language Hacking Guide** from Benny Lewis

Chapter 13:

- **Travel Hacking Cartel** from Chris Guillebeau

- **Oneworld,** consisting of American Airlines, British Airways, Cathay Pacific, Iberia, LAN, Qantas, and several others.

- **Star Alliance** which consists of United, Continental, US Airways, Lufthansa, Swiss, and several more.

- **Skyteam** which consists of Delta, Air France, KLM, and many others.

- **Credit Karma** for monitoring your credit rating

- **Chase Sapphire Preferred**

- **Amex Starwood Preferred Guest**

- **Citi Platinum Select**

- Chris Guilleabeau's **Card For Travel site.**

- **Tripadvisor** and **TripIt** application for travel planning and reviews

- **Hipmunk** and **Airfarewatchdog** for travel bookings

- **Flightfox** outsourcing flight search engine platform

- **Flight Tracker** flight tracking and flight status application

- **Airport Transit** Guide is a traveler's complete guide to some 460 airports around the world, covering just about all the options for airport access.

- **Gate Guru** will help you navigate through unfamiliar airports so you're not left running to your gate.

- **Weather Channel** gives you the weather forecast, both local and international so you can plan ahead weeks, days or even hours.

- **Weather Bug has more than** 35,000 monitoring stations worldwide, so you can get access to hyper-local weather updates.

- **Google Maps** online or via a smartphone app is free and you get turn-by-turn GPS navigation for driving, walking, public transport and sometimes bike routes.

- **HopStop** gives you door-to-door public transit directions for Subway, Train, Bus, ferry, Bike & Taxi for all of the US, Canada, UK, France, Australia, New Zealand and Russia.

- **Uber** acts as your private driver (in the US and Canada only, for now) and **MyTaxi** allows you to book taxi drivers and rate and review drivers.

- **WhatGas** allows you to find the cheapest prices on petrol or gas in several countries around the world. **Gas Buddy** works in Canada and the US.

- **Couchsurfing** allows you to stay with hosts around the world for free.

- **Hostels.com, hostelbookers.com** and **hostelworld.com** for cheap accommodation

- **MindMyHouse.com, housesitworld.com** or **trustedhousesitter.com**.

- Vacation rental sites **Home Exchange, Intervac,** or **IHEN**

- **Airbnb** connects travelers with places to stay, that aren't as expensive as hotels, and are more like renting your own apartment or house.

- **Agoda** and **Priceline** offer big discounts on hotels.

- **Expedia** has great deals on flights and hotels

- **Living Social** or **Groupon** offer daily deals on things to do and see in a city

- **Luxury Hotels of the World**

- **Yelp** and **Foodspotting** help you find great food and share ratings and reviews

- **Akamai's State of the Internet' report** for Q1 2013

- **Free Wi-Fi Finder** lets you search for free Internet Hotspots anywhere in the world, both online and off.

- **Skype Wi-Fi** allows you to get online at over 1 million Wi-Fi hotspots worldwide

- **What's App** is a free app you install on your smartphone that allows you to text message anyone for free and send photos when you have Wi-Fi or data

- **DOODAD** is a data-only travel SIM card which you put into your unlocked smartphone or tablet, to gain access to pre-paid data (which lasts a year).

- **Private Wi-Fi** is a virtual private network service (VPN) that encrypts your communications

- **TrustGo Antivirus & Mobile Security** is the best free app to secure your Android.

- **Prey Project** is a feature-rich and stable open-source program to protect your laptop's contents

- **SKRoss World Adapator Pro + USB** travel adaptor

- **Lifetrons High Tech Multi-Tool Adaptor.**

- **Lifetrons High Performance Digital Power Charger** claims to be the world's smallest high capacity portable charger.

- **Anker® Astro Pro2 20000mAh External Battery Charger** can power your tablet, netbook, notebook, laptop and smartphone.

- **Powerbag Business Class Pack** is the ultimate wearable solution, as a backpack with a built-in battery system

- **Mophie Juice Pack Plus** is a really cool, fully protective, form-fitting case with an extended, built-in rechargeable battery for your iPhone and the **PowerSkin Protective Case with Built-in Battery** does the same for Motorola DROID X and DROID X2.

- **Seagate Backup Plus** and **My Passport Essential SE** external hard drives

- **EatSmart Precision Voyager Digital Luggage Scale.**

- **1Above** is your inflight drink to cure or decrease jetlag, especially on those long-haul flights.

- **Espanol Podcast**, **Daily French Pod**, **Learn Italian Pod**, **My German Class** and **Learn Chinese Pod** for language learning podcasts.

- **Teach Yourself** and **Anki** are language learning resources

About the Author

Natalie Sisson is a New Zealand entrepeneur and adventurer who lives in her suitcase, traveling the world and running her business, while ensuring she helps others to create freedom in business and adventure in life. She's dedicated to playing Ultimate Frisbee, singing and dancing wherever possible and and pushing her boundaries.

She's the author of:

- BYOB Build Your Online Business

- How to Crowd Fund Your Dream Idea on Kickstarter

- 25 Lessons Learned From Being In Business Manifesto

If you want to get really useful business and lifestyle tips that you can actually put into action then sign up to the weekly Highflyer newsletter at **suitcaseentrepeneur.com/freedom**.

You can read the Suitcase Entrepreneur Blog packed with articles, videos and podcast episodes on creating your ideal lifestyle and a thriving online business at **suitcaseentrepreneur.com/entrepreneurs-blog**

Plus you can connect with Natalie on Twitter @suitcasepreneur, **facebook. com/suitcaseentrepreneur** and **youtube.com/nataliesisson** and many more social media sites from her website **suitcaseentrepreneur.com**.

While you're at it you can download her mobile app on iTunes and GooglePlay for fresh content and the latest products and events as she'd love to meet you on her journey around the world.

Acknowledgements

"50 years from now when you're looking back at your life, don't you wanna be able to say you had the guts to do it?"
~SAM WITWICKI

I knew all those years of writing copious amounts of thoughts and experiences in my personal diaries would someday account for something, or that reading every single Famous Five book from Enid Blyton and epic adventure novel from Wilbur Smith, would amount to something one day.

Writing and publishing this book has been a personal childhood dream of mine that I finally reclaimed and you wouldn't be reading it without the support of a dedicated team of people who believed that it should be written.

I truly appreciate the master wordsmith, Matthew Kimberley who had no idea that I'd ask him to step up as Chief Editor on a ridiculously tight turnaround time, after doing such a fantastic job editing my personal story in Chapter 1, while still keeping its essence.

This book was made infinitely better by your brilliant skills as an author and copywriter to trim down my tendency for verboseness, and because you're one of the funniest friends and accountability partners I've ever had.

Of course, before it even got to Matthew it went through rounds of editing from my Kickstarter Editorial team who I'd like to thank for paying to become my editors! Special shout outs go to Ed Sharlow, James Wightman, Inga Spouse and Yasmine Khater who consistently read every single chapter as it was released to provide much appreciated feedback and amendments.

Also thank you to the Guillaume Ceccarelli (also for making the very first supporting pledge to this book), Prime Sarmiento, Beverlee Rasmussen, Stephanie Katcher, Karen Martin, Nancy Lynn, Pamela Slim, Caroline Ceniza-Levine, Kylie Pengelly, Ashok Amaran, and Sandy Gerber.

Roger Boyd, Alexis Neely, Kieran McDonogh and Liz Dickinson your sponsorship generosity knows no bounds. Thank you for your belief.

Kyle Durand, without your knowledge and wisdom my chapter on setting up an international business would be completely unfounded.

Thanks to artistic talents of Sarah Steeland for providing the original travel bug artwork to visually represent the three acts in this book.

To all the amazing members of my Suitcase Entrepreneur community and book marketing group, for often being more enthusiastic than I was during the writing of my book, and for the hundreds of comments and feedback on cover designs, taglines, quotes and topics to cover. It is always fun to crowd source a project when people truly give a damn.

Big thanks to Jenny Blake for inspiring me to get this book out into the world over two years ago when you shared your book proposal with me so that I could start my own, and for answering all my many questions on what it really takes to write a book.

Gratitude also goes out to Chris Guillebeau, Jonathan Fields and David Fugate for your advice, guidance and honesty along the way, as well as Pam Slim for sharing your personal writing tips on the high seas of the Caribbean.

Big ups to my man Chris Ducker for providing the brainstorming sessions in the Philippines on how to make both our books the best they possibly could be and for your continual support in my journey.

To my ladies, Natalie MacNeil and Marianne Cantwell, thank you for keeping it real in our many conversations on the whole book publishing process.

Much thanks to Alex Reyes for making my book website look hot, Cher Hale for making the book tour come to fruition, Tia Lloyd for the fantastic merchandise and enthusiasm and Mike Bruny for your hip hop affirmations.

Full credit goes to Alexander von Ness for the beautiful cover design and Laura Brady for the typesetting and interior layout. Huge thanks to Cheryl Wood for stepping in to take over the precise task of converting this book design to be read and loved on any device.

Paul Jeffery and Michael Cook at Enthrill for the collaboration on the cool book cards and Tia Lloyd for the merchandise for my world book tour.

I'd be remiss to not thank Seth Godin for having the most influence on my work and life over the years, and for taking the time to meet me in person and encourage me to be a Linchpin.

I'm grateful to the countless friends who supported me on this journey and gave me the momentum when I was struggling to find it, even though they still don't really understand exactly what I do (although perhaps after reading this book they finally will).

To all of you included in this book in one way or another, thank you so much for allowing me to share your stories, case studies and insights – this book is richer for it.

And finally to my father Peter, whose love of the English language and daily crosswords sparked my curiosity for how to make an impact through stories and the power of words. This is just the beginning.

*-Natalie Sisson, **Chief Adventurer and Freedom Seeker.***